EXPERIENCING SUCCESS
GOD'S WAY

EXPERIENCING SUCCESS
GOD'S WAY

CHARLES
STANLEY

OLIVER
NELSON ™

THOMAS NELSON PUBLISHERS
Nashville

Published in Nashville, Tennessee, by Thomas Nelson, Inc.

Unless otherwise noted, Scripture quotations are from THE NEW KING
JAMES VERSION. Copyright © 1979, 1980, 1982, Thomas Nelson, Inc.,
Publishers.

Scriptures noted NASB are taken from the NEW AMERICAN STANDARD
BIBLE, Copyright © The Lockman Foundation 1960, 1962, 1963, 1968,
1971, 1972, 1973, 1975, 1977. Used by permission.

ISBN 0-7852-7292-5

Printed in the United States of America
01 02 03 04 05 06 07 QPV 05 04 03 02 01 00

CONTENTS

GOD WANTS YOU TO EXPERIENCE SUCCESS!

Some people are just born to be successful."

"A Christian can't really be a successful person—too many worldly things are required if a person is going to achieve major success."

"God is interested in many things, but my success isn't one of them."

"I'm not sure I can count on God to help me succeed in reaching my goals."

If you hold any of these attitudes, I want to share this good news with you. God *does* desire for you to be successful. He is deeply committed to your success, if you are willing to pursue success *His* way and to adopt *His* definition of success. And yes, Christians can be successful—including *you*.

Success does not belong only to those who are born with a certain degree of privilege or who achieve a basic level of education or social acceptance. Neither is success automatically to be associated with lying, cheating, dishonesty, or other actions that are apart from God's commandments for Christian living.

Rather, success is God's plan for Christians. Furthermore, most of the concepts the world calls "principles for success" are actually ones based upon God's Word.

God's Definition of Success

At the very outset of this study guide, I believe it is important for us to define success from God's perspective and to compare that definition with the world's definition.

From the world's perspective, success is subject to a great deal of individual interpretation. A football coach might define success as winning a national championship. A college student might define success as earning a degree . . . a salesman, as being number one in the company . . . a parent, as raising godly children.

Definitions come and go, depending on whom you ask and when you ask. Generally speaking, many people define success as "setting a goal and accomplishing it."

That definition, however, is very limited. A person might set an evil goal or a good goal. The *nature* of the goals we set is a key factor in success, and especially so, if we are dealing with God's view of success.

As Christians, our goals must not be defined in terms of "my will," but rather our goals must be rooted in what we know to be "God's will." Our human approach tends to say: "Here's what I want to do and what I want to accomplish." A Christian's approach must be: "Here is what I believe God wants me to be and to do, and here's how I can become that type of person and accomplish those tasks." The Christian faces the challenge of *being* a godly person, then *obeying* God in His directives.

Our life as Christians is not to be wrapped up in what we earn or own. Life for the Christian is wrapped up in who we *are* in Christ Jesus.

The definition of success on which this study guide is based is this:

> Success is to continue desiring to be the person God has called me to be and to achieve those goals that God has helped me to set.

Can an ungodly person be genuinely successful according to this definition? No. An ungodly person might amass a certain degree of material wealth, achieve a certain degree of fame, gain a certain number of degrees or awards, attain a certain level of social privilege or status, or acquire a certain degree of political or social power, but the ungodly person cannot be truly successful in his life because he does not desire to be the *person* God has called him to be. He is achieving *his* goals, not God's goals. He is defining his life according to his own lusts, desires, and purposes rather than seeking to line up his life with God's desires, plans, and purposes.

The world tends to sum up success as fame and fortune. God sums up success in terms of relationship, character, and obedience. He desires for us to succeed first and foremost in our relationship with Him, then in our relationships with others, and then in our vocations and ministries. The godly person who is pursuing God's plan and purposes for his life certainly may experience wealth, prominence, and status as side benefits, but these are not to be the Christian's primary goals and objectives.

The True Rewards of God-Based Success

The true rewards associated with God's success are the intangibles that *all* people want. The self-focused person may think he desires fame and fortune. But in the end, every person has as his or her deepest desire inner peace, joy, contentment, health and wholeness (spirit, mind, and body), feelings of spiritual security, the hope of eternal life, family love, and a living relationship with God. On more than one occasion, I have heard a wealthy or famous person who is considered to be successful by others say, "I'd trade it all for a little tranquility and a secure hope that I know what is going to happen to me after I die." I have heard so-called successful people say, "I'd trade everything I have acquired and earned for an hour of pure love, an hour without pain, or an hour of knowing that I have done what God created me to do."

Those who limit their pursuit in life only to fame and fortune wind up frustrated, disappointed, and, in the end, with a gaping void in their lives that they cannot fill. Those who choose first to pursue the life for which God designed them and to which God calls them are those who experience the real "richness" of life and the hope of everlasting life.

The Most Important Question You Can Ask

The most important question you can ask about your success is this: "What is it that the Lord wants me to be and to do today?"

That is not only a question to ask once, but a question to ask every day. Success, according to our definition above, is an *ongoing pursuit.* It is establishing and accomplishing and forever seeking to establish and accomplish the God-given goals the Lord sets for our lives. It is refusing to become discouraged, disheartened, or dissuaded from God's goals. It is a *continuing* desire to be the person God calls us to be and to achieve the goals that God helps us to set.

Just as no person can ever reach the horizon, so no person can ever truly achieve success. Success is not a quantity that can be measured or a concept that can be fully defined. Success is a concept embedded in a *process.* Our understanding of success grows as we mature in Christ. It is something that continually lies ahead of us and continually develops within us.

The Holy Spirit works in us in a unique way. He allows us to experience great joy and satisfaction in the present moment of our lives, and at the same time, He calls us to yet greater conformity to Christ Jesus, to greater desires for ministry, and to greater tasks in the establishing of God's purposes on the earth.

The genuine Christian always has a hunger in his heart to be more like Christ, to draw nearer to the heart of God, and to know more about the truth God presents in His Word. A genuine Christian always has a thirst to experience more of the goodness of God, to serve Him with greater consistency and effectiveness, and to bear more and more eternal fruit.

The quest to satisfy that hunger and thirst is the quest of success. It is a lifelong quest. It is also the most satisfying way a person might ever live.

What Is Your Desire Today?

Genuine success—from God's point of view—is rooted in what God sets as the goals for our lives. It is rooted in the relationship God desires to have with us. It begins within us the moment we say to the Lord, "It's not what I want to be that matters—it's who You want me to be. It's not what I want to do that counts—it's what You want me to do that is my goal."

What are your desires today regarding your own success? What are your answers to these three key questions:

1. Do you truly desire to be a success from God's point of view?
2. Do you desire to be all that God calls you to be in Christ Jesus?
3. Do you desire to do all that the Lord directs you to do on a day-to-day basis?

ONE

DEFINING SUCCESS— GOD'S WAY

Countless books on success are on the market today. I've probably read two or three bookshelves worth of such books. Some of the authors have included God in their discussion of success, and a few have even put God at the center of a successful life. One thing I discovered in reading these books, however, is that without exception, every genuine success principle they describe can be found in the Bible. The principles of genuine success are not foreign to a godly life—rather, they are embedded in a godly life.

The world may think it has discovered this idea or that idea about success, but in truth, God is the author of all success and the Bible is the foremost "success book" you can ever read.

One of the key words that the Bible uses to describe success is *prosperity*. To prosper in all you do is to succeed in all you do. To be prosperous is to be successful. Any time we read in the Bible about the Lord prospering His people, we can be assured that the Lord is helping His people to succeed in all ways.

Another key concept related to Bible prosperity is *whole-person prosperity*. We read in 3 John 2, "Beloved, I pray that you may prosper in all things and be in health, just as your soul prospers." To prosper in all things is to prosper materially, socially, naturally, financially, materially, and also to prosper emotionally, spiritually, and in every creative endeavor.

God desires for the success principles of His Word to touch every aspect of your life—your spiritual walk, finances, vocation, service to the Lord, health, and relationships with family members and friends.

A third Bible concept about success that is important to recognize as you begin this study is this: We are told that we, as the Lord's followers, will prosper outwardly *as our souls prosper.* Inner prosperity and success and wholeness lead to outer prosperity, success, and wholeness.

Many people approach success from the outside in. They look at the external trappings of success and conclude that a person surely must be experiencing inner peace, joy, hope, love, and faith. Not so. Genuine success begins on the inside and works its way out.

How many of us truly want to prosper to the degree that our souls are prospering? I suspect very few. Most people are seeking to prosper in their finances and material lives with very little regard to their souls prospering. The challenge of the Bible is to place greater emphasis on the *inner* state of our prosperity than on the outer. The challenge is to grow spiritually, and as we do, the outer manifestations of prosperity will appear in the form of fruitfulness and blessing.

Furthermore, the degree to which we prosper spiritually will be in *direct proportion* to the degree we will prosper materially, in our work, and in our relationships.

As you study God's principles for prosperity and success, I encourage you to go again and again to your Bible and to underline phrases, highlight words or verses, and make notes in the margins of your Bible to record the specific ways God speaks to you. My Bible is well-marked with dates, notes, and insights. It is a "living reference" for me regarding God's plans and purposes for my success in life.

God's truth is for all people at all times, but the application of God's truth to your life is always personal and direct. Take note of the specific ways in which God admonishes, encourages, or directs you. The principles of success in God's Word do not change. But the *application* of those principles is always highly individualized under the direction of the Holy Spirit. Be aware as you read and study God's Word that His Word is eternal, but also timely . . . universal, but also personal . . . absolute truth, but also practical in providing day-to-day advice as you face the unique situations and circumstances of your life.

For Personal or Group Study

This book can be used for small-group study or for personal study. If you are using this book for a personal Bible study, you will find places from time to time in which to note your insights or to respond to questions that are asked. If you are using the book for a small-group study, you also may use these questions and insight portions for group discussion.

At various times you will be asked to respond to the material in one of these ways:

- What new insights have you gained?
- Have you ever had a similar experience?
- How do you feel about the material presented?
- In what way do you feel challenged to respond or to act?

Insights

An insight is an "aha" moment regarding the meaning and application of the Bible. An insight is more than a mere fact or idea. It is seeing something as if it is new to you.

Most of us have had the experience of reading a passage of the Bible—perhaps dozens of times—and then suddenly saying one day, "I never saw *that* before!" It may be a particular word or phrase that seems to leap from the page with added meaning, giving a new understanding to a particular story or teaching. That is a spiritual insight.

Your insights are likely to be highly individualized and are often related to your personal life. They come as you relate what you are currently experiencing or encountering to the light of God's Word. At other times, an insight may help you pull together your random reflections about a relationship, experience, or incident. At still other times, an insight may provide a cohesive answer to a question with which you have been struggling—you may have new understanding about what to do, how to think, or how to believe.

Ask the Lord to speak to you personally every time you open your Bible to read and study it. I believe He will be faithful in answering your prayer.

As you experience insights, make notes about them. Write them in the margins of your Bible or in a separate journal. I suggest this for two reasons: (1) The more you record insights, the more you are likely to have insights. It seems the more people look and listen for God to speak to them, the more He does! (2) In times of frustration, discouragement, doubt, or struggle, you will find it helpful to look back through your Bible or journal to see what the Lord has revealed to you in the past as His specific word to you. Your faith will grow. Your understanding will deepen. And I believe you will also experience the personal presence of God in a renewed way.

As you record your insights, make sure you are recording *your* personal response or insight, not just summarizing what someone else or your small group as a whole may have concluded. For an insight to be valid, it must be *your* insight.

Experience

We each come to God's Word from a unique background. Nobody else has our particular set of experiences, relationships, or contexts for learning. We each come to God's Word with a bank of ideas, opinions, and emotions. Therefore, we each have a unique perspective on what we read in the Bible.

Differing levels of experience may create problems in group Bible studies, although this is not necessarily so. Those who have gone to church all their lives or who have heard a great deal of teaching about God's principles for success may come to a study on success from a different perspective than a new believer who is encountering the Bible's success principles for the first time. Make sure that you acknowledge and accept different levels of experience in your group. No person should be made to feel left out.

Recognize, too, that what we hold in common in any group setting are "life experiences." We each can point to times in our lives in which we have found the Bible to be applicable to us—perhaps in a convicting or challenging way, perhaps in an encouraging or comforting way. We have had experiences that caused us to conclude, "Here's how the truth of that passage manifested itself in my life."

Of course, our experiences do not make the Bible true. The Bible is truth, period. But our unique experiences do reveal how God's truth can be *applied* in special, personal ways. Our experiences point out God's awesome, unending creativity in dealing with each person individually and lovingly. We learn through sharing with others how God's Word can be applied to very practical needs, questions, and situations.

Sharing experiences is significant for spiritual growth. The person who *shares* an experience grows in his ability to give testimony to God's goodness. The person who *hears* another person share an experience grows in empathy and in understanding. If you are doing this study on your own, find someone with whom you can share your faith experiences. In return, be open to hearing about what the Lord has done in his or her life.

Emotional Response

Just as we each come to God's Word with a unique set of life experiences, so we come to the Bible with our own set of emotional responses. What causes one person to feel encouragement or joy may cause another person to feel confusion, frustration, or conviction.

In dealing with the topic of success, one person may be very eager to experience success and approach success with the attitude, "I want all God has for me!" Another person may approach success with great caution, reserve, and even doubt, saying, "I'm not all that sure a Christian *should* be successful." Yet a third person may say, "Well, I'm all for success . . . but too much of it is probably not good for a Christian." Can enthusiasm for success, doubt about success, and caution regarding success coexist as responses in the same group? Yes—especially if you recognize that these are essentially *emotional responses* toward the topic of success more than they are rational, objective conclusions that are directly drawn from God's Word. The underlying foundation for each of these responses is related to emotions a person feels regarding God's love, grace, mercy, judgment, and commandments.

Allow each person in your group to express his or her emotional response *without judgment*. No one emotional response is "right." Count every emotional expression as valuable, to both the hearers and the speaker.

Face your own emotions honestly. Learn to share your emotional responses with others. It may take courage for you to express an emotional response—if so, be courageous!

Ask yourself such questions as these:

- How do you feel when an ungodly person seems to be successful in the material and financial world, while a godly person seems to struggle materially or financially?
- How do you feel when you work hard and yet are not "rewarded" externally for your efforts?
- How do you feel when you read God's promises about prosperity?
- How do you feel when others tell you to be "patient" regarding success?

• How do you feel when a person tells you that a Christian can never be successful?

A lack of prosperity can cause a person to feel discouraged, fearful, anxious, and frustrated. Total provision and prosperity, on the other hand, can cause a person to feel elated, joyful, energetic, creative, hopeful, satisfied, and fulfilled. As a person moves from poverty to prosperity, issues associated with pride, greed, and envy may emerge. Own up to these emotions! Explore them. Discover God's truth related to them.

Guard yourselves continually against a tendency to feel guilty about a lack of prosperity, or to feel smug about ways in which you have experienced prosperity.

Emotional responses do not give validity to the Scriptures. Nor should you trust emotions as a measuring device for your faith. Your faith must be based on what God says, not on how you feel. The value of recognizing emotional responses is that they provide a starting place for growth.

When we acknowledge an emotional response, we are in a much better position to explore the reasons underlying that emotional response. As we explore God's Word about our emotional response, and then seek God's forgiveness, remedy, or approval of our emotional response, we become more conformed to Christ. We *grow* spiritually. And spiritual growth should be the desired outcome for any Bible study!

In most small-group settings, I have found that it is much more beneficial for people to express emotions rather than opinions. Opinions tend to divide and to alienate. The sharing of emotional responses tends to unite and create empathy within a group. When we are vulnerable in sharing our feelings with one another, we open ourselves up to the work of the Holy Spirit in our lives. A sense of community develops, and we understand more clearly what it means to be "one in the Spirit." It is through the sharing of joys and sorrows, assurances and doubts, hopes and fears, that we mature as individuals and as churches.

Challenges

Our experiences and emotional responses are unique. So, too, are the challenges we experience as the result of studying God's Word. As we read and study the Bible on any topic, we inevitably come to a point of conviction. God seems to be speaking directly to us about something He desires for us to change, to do, or to strengthen.

God's Word may challenge you to make a fresh start in your life, to stand firm or continue steadfastly in the direction you are going, or to alter your thinking on a particular topic. These moments of conviction can be very strong. They may occur once or repeatedly, but they are virtually impossible to escape or ignore completely.

The more practical the subject matter, the stronger the conviction seems to be. Perhaps that is because God's message and meaning are so clear that there is little room to justify, explain away, or misinterpret what God is saying to you.

I am saying this to alert you to the fact that as you study God's Word regarding success and prosperity, you are likely to feel challenged or convicted in rather powerful ways. Your first impulse may be to close your Bible, close this book, and walk away—feeling either elated or deflated! Don't give in to that impulse. Stay with your study and get the whole of God's message.

Many people seem to pick out two or three verses on success and call them their own. They often isolate these verses from the context of the Scriptures as a whole, and in that, they make a serious error. God's Word is to be taken as a whole. Concepts build upon concepts. Truths reinforce truths. What we are aiming at in this Bible study is a look at the "whole" of God's message on success. While we cannot cover every verse in the Bible on this subject matter, we are aiming at an understanding of God's teaching as a whole.

I believe a person can gain a great deal by writing down specific ways in which he is feeling stretched, molded, called, or convicted by God. When we identify clearly and succinctly what God wants us to do and *why*, we are in a much better position to take action that is responsible, measured, and deliberate. We are to *respond* to God's Word, not merely react to it.

God desires us to get into His Word so that His Word can get into us . . . and in turn, so that we might *apply* His Word to our lives. We are to live out God's Word in all we say and do, and in the process, be witnesses to God's love, mercy, and help. We are to be "living letters" about God's plan for success and prosperity. It is not enough for us to note our insights, recall our past experiences, share our emotions, or write down the ways in which we feel challenged. We must actually *do* what God calls us to do. We must obey God's Word and be doers of it (see James 1:22).

Specifically, it isn't enough for you to become savvy about success. God calls you to *be* successful from the inside out.

Keep the Bible Central

I encourage you to keep the Bible at the center of your study. Don't stray into what this expert or that success-guru has to say. A small-group study on success too easily can result in a financial-advice session. Stay focused on God's Word. Let God use His Word to speak directly to each heart.

If you are doing a personal Bible study, you also must be diligent in staying focused on God's Word. Keep in mind always that growing into the fullness of the stature of Christ Jesus is the goal. After all, Jesus was *the* most successful person who ever lived on this earth!

Prayer

I also encourage you to begin and end your Bible study sessions in prayer. Ask God to give you spiritual eyes to see what He wants you to see and spiritual ears to hear what He wants you to hear. Ask Him to give you new insights, to recall to your memory the experiences that are most helpful to your growth, and to help you identify your emotions clearly. Be bold in asking the Lord to reveal to you what He desires for you to do. Be sensitive to the next step you should take as you walk out His success plan for your life.

As you conclude a time of study, ask the Lord to seal to your heart and mind what you have learned so that you will never forget it. Ask Him to transform you more into the likeness of Christ Jesus every day. Ask Him to help you become truly successful in His eyes.

The Depth of God's Word

Make success an ongoing study in your life. After ten lessons on this topic, you will have only begun to explore all that God desires to teach you on this topic. You'll find evidence and examples related to prosperity in virtually every story in the Bible. Continue to grow and to apply what the Lord has revealed to you about success. As you receive blessing from the Lord, seek out practical and specific ways in which you might be a greater blessing to those around you.

• *What questions do you presently have regarding success and God's desire for you to be successful? Is there something specific you hope to gain from this study?*

_____

_____

• *In what areas do you feel you are lacking or are failing to experience prosperity and success?*

_____

_____

• *How do you feel about success? How do you feel when you hear someone say to you, "God wants you to be more successful"?*

_____

_____

• *Do you truly desire to be successful from God's perspective?*

_____

_____

TWO

GOD'S COMMITMENT TO YOUR SUCCESS

G od not only desires your success, but He is *committed* to helping His people become successful. He desires for His people to be blessed and to experience whole-person prosperity.

Nehemiah was a man in the Bible who believed and claimed God's success for himself. When he heard news that the walls and gates of Jerusalem lay in ruins, he began to fast and pray about the situation. The king noticed his sorrow, and upon hearing the reason for Nehemiah's sadness, the king authorized Nehemiah to go to Jerusalem and make repairs to the city.

When Nehemiah arrived in Jerusalem, he immediately faced opposition from those who did not want him to succeed in the task before him. He responded to those who opposed him by saying:

> The God of heaven Himself will prosper us; therefore we His servants will arise and build, but you have no heritage or right or memorial in Jerusalem. (Neh. 2:20)

• *Are you firmly convinced today that God desires for you to prosper?*

_____

_____

• *Are there specific reasons why you believe God will not cause you to prosper? Are these reasons related to sin or to the pursuit of a goal that is contrary to God's commandments? Are these reasons related to your feelings of failure, your past experience with failure, or your belief that only some of God's children should prosper?*

_____

_____

What the Word Says

Then Peter opened his mouth and said: "In truth I perceive that God shows no partiality. But in every nation whoever fears Him and works righteousness is accepted by Him." (Acts 10:34–35)

Beloved, I pray that you may prosper in all things and be in health, just as your soul prospers. (3 John 2)

Let them shout
for joy and be glad,
Who favor my righteous cause;
And let them say continually,
"Let the LORD be magnified,
Who has pleasure in the prosperity of
His servant." (Ps. 35:27)

What the Word Says to Me

_____

_____

_____

_____

_____

_____

_____

_____

_____

_____

_____

_____

_____

_____

_____

_____

_____

_____

_____

Four Basic Aspects of God's Commitment to Your Success

The Bible presents four basic concepts that are important for you to grasp if you are to understand God's commitment to your success.

1. God desires for you to live successfully regardless of your outer circumstances. Perhaps no person in the Bible experienced more difficult circumstances in his life—for his entire life— than Daniel. Daniel was taken captive by the Babylonians when he was a young man. He was forced to live in an alien culture the rest of his life and to serve three heathen kings— Nebuchadnezzar, Cyrus, and Darius. On several occasions, Daniel had to stand in opposition to the king's magicians. On one occasion, his opposition resulted in his facing a den of lions. Yet we read in Daniel 6:28, "So this Daniel prospered in the reign of Darius and in the reign of Cyrus the Persian." Daniel lived well and lived successfully *in the midst of his circumstances.* We are called to do the same.

Too often we look at our outward circumstances and we conclude, "God must not want to prosper me." We must never look to outward circumstances, including our past failures, and use them as a reason to doubt God's desire to prosper us. True prosperity begins in the heart and soul of a person. True prosperity is *always* a possibility for us because change and spiritual growth are always possible for the Christian.

2. Your success is directly related to your faith. For a person to be successful, a person must first *believe* he or she can be successful. The real question for the Christian is, "Believe in what? Have faith in whom?" When we identify the object of our faith, we truly know the *foundation* for our success. If you are putting your faith in God to help you define and become a success, then your foundation is as strong as He is!

• *Do you BELIEVE today that God WILL lead you to greater success in your life?*

_____

_____

What the Word Says	**What the Word Says to Me**
Without faith it is impossible to please Him, for he who comes to God must believe that He is, and that He is a rewarder of those who diligently seek Him. (Heb. 11:6)	----------------------------------- ----------------------------------- ----------------------------------- ----------------------------------- -----------------------------------
If any of you lacks wisdom [or any other aspect of whole-person success], let him ask of God, who gives to all liberally and without reproach, and it will be given to him. But let him ask in faith, with no doubting, for he who doubts is like a wave of the sea driven and tossed by the wind. For let not that man suppose that he will receive anything from the Lord; he is a double-minded man, unstable in all his ways. (James 1:5–8)	----------------------------------- ----------------------------------- ----------------------------------- ----------------------------------- ----------------------------------- ----------------------------------- ----------------------------------- ----------------------------------- ----------------------------------- ----------------------------------- ----------------------------------- -----------------------------------

3. God's commitment to our success is related to our courage and to our obedience in keeping His commandments. As Joshua prepared to lead the Israelites across the Jordan River to claim the Promised Land, God spoke these words to him:

Be strong and very courageous, that you may observe to do according to all the law which Moses My servant commanded you; do not turn from it to the right hand or to the left, that you may prosper wherever you go. This Book of the Law shall not depart from your mouth, but you shall meditate in it day and night, that you may observe to do according to all that is written in it. For then you will make your way prosperous, and then you will have good success. Have I not commanded you? Be strong and of good courage; do not be afraid, nor be dismayed, for the LORD your God is with you wherever you go. (Josh. 1:7–9)

The issue for Christians is not whether God is committed to their success, but, rather, whether we are committed to keeping God's commandments, having courage, using our faith, and choosing to believe for success regardless of the outer circumstances of our lives.

•*What new insights do you have into Joshua 1:7–9?*

_____

_____

• *Can you recall experiences in your life when your failing to obey God's commandments, failing to use your faith, or failing to have courage led to a lack of success?*

_____

_____

4. *The Bible presents success as a process, not a destination.* Living successfully does not mean that you are going to live on the top of the mountain with a big grin on your face and a blue ribbon attached to your lapel every moment of every day of your life. High points may come. They may be frequent at times and virtually nonexistent at other times.

Success is to be found in the *way* in which we live out our lives day in and day out. It is to be found as we *pursue* what God calls us to be and to do. Success is not the end of a process. It is *how we undertake the process called life.*

• *How do you feel about these principles related to your success?*

_____

_____

Four Reasons We Can Know
God Desires Success for Us

God gives us abundant evidence in His Word that He desires for us to be successful. We see that evidence in at least four areas:

1. Each of us has a built-in desire for success. Every baby comes into this world goal-oriented. He has a built-in desire to get his needs met and to take control of his world. He has a desire to learn to communicate and to become mobile—to scoot, to crawl, to walk.

God has built a desire for success into us so we will *act.* This drive in us can motivate us toward the pursuit of the things of God or the things of our own flesh (the lust of the flesh, the lust of the eyes, and the pride of life—see 1 John 2:16). It is up to us how we will choose to act on the built-in desire God gives us toward success, satisfaction, and fulfillment.

What the Word Says	What the Word Says to Me
As he thinks in his heart, so is he. (Prov. 23:7)	---------------------------------- ----------------------------------
Hear, my son, and be wise; And guide your heart in the way. (Prov. 23:19)	---------------------------------- ---------------------------------- ----------------------------------
Depart from evil and do good; Seek peace and pursue it. (Ps. 34:14)	---------------------------------- ---------------------------------- ----------------------------------

2. God has equipped you for success. God has given you one or more natural talents and abilities, as well as one or more spiritual gifts. These gifts have been grafted into your unique personality for one reason—so that you might use these gifts to the best of your ability and produce quality work that has a potential for both earthly and eternal reward. It is up to each of us to discover our gifts and then to develop them to the best of our ability. That takes practice and discipline—both of which God provides to us when we ask.

What the Word Says	What the Word Says to Me
Now may He who supplies seed to the sower, and bread for food, supply and multiply the seed you have sown and increase the fruits of your righteousness. (2 Cor. 9:10)	--------------------------- --------------------------- --------------------------- --------------------------- --------------------------- ---------------------------
They glorify God for the obedience of your confession to the gospel of Christ, and for your liberal sharing with them and all men . . . the exceeding grace of God in you. Thanks be to God for His indescribable gift! (2 Cor. 9:13–15)	--------------------------- --------------------------- --------------------------- --------------------------- --------------------------- --------------------------- ---------------------------
Every good gift and every perfect gift is from above, and comes down from the Father of lights. (James 1:17)	--------------------------- --------------------------- --------------------------- ---------------------------

3. The Lord has given us His Holy Spirit to help us succeed. The Holy Spirit has been given to every believer to

- perfect our gifts,
- give strength to us in our areas of weakness, and
- to give us daily guidance or "counsel" into the ways in which we should go, including the decisions we

should make, the choices we should make, and the opportunities we should pursue.

The Holy Spirit works within us to renew our strength, sharpen our senses, and help us get the most amount of work done in the most efficient manner.

It is the Holy Spirit who causes the use of our gifts to be effective in helping or blessing others. The Holy Spirit also directs us toward those who need what we have been equipped to give. When we yield ourselves and our gifts to the Holy Spirit, it is the Holy Spirit who comforts us and reassures us that all things *are* working together for our good from God's perspective (Rom. 8:28).

The Holy Spirit is God's gift to us to *enable* our success.

What the Word Says	What the Word Says to Me
Read Daniel 3 and focus particularly on this verse:	----------------------------------
Our God whom we serve is able. (Dan. 3:17)	----------------------------------
[Jesus said,] "When He, the Spirit of truth, has come, He will guide you into all truth." (John 16:13)	----------------------------------
Likewise the Spirit also helps in our weaknesses. (Rom. 8:26)	----------------------------------
He who is in you is greater than he who is in the world. (1 John 4:4)	----------------------------------

Never dismiss or diminish the value of what the Lord has given you for your success.

We must refuse to discount the gifts we have been given, which is what we do when we say things such as

- "My race is against me."
- "I don't have enough formal education."
- "I was born at the wrong time on the wrong side of the tracks."
- "I'm too old."
- "I've got circumstances that will forever keep me from being successful."

God has uniquely gifted you to be a success in a unique calling He has for your life. No excuse is justified in His presence. In whatever area you may feel weak or inadequate, His presence and power are more than sufficient!

> • *Have you been using excuses for your lack of success? Are you willing to admit that the Holy Spirit in you is greater than any weakness or inhibiting factor you may have in your life?*

_____

_____

4. God has given you the power of prayer so you might use it to further your success. Every one of us has the privilege of bowing before God every morning of our lives and saying, "Lord, I need Your help. I need Your guidance. I need Your strength and wisdom." The Lord delights in our prayers that request His help. He delights in our prayers that are expressions of our faith in Him to help us succeed at what He calls us to be and to do. Prayer is a powerful tool that God intends for you to use in becoming *all* that He desires for you to be.

What the Word Says	What the Word Says to Me
The effective, fervent prayer of a righteous man avails much. Elijah was a man with a nature	_____ _____ _____

like ours, and he prayed
earnestly that it would not rain;
and it did not rain on the land
for three years and six months.
And he prayed again, and the
heaven gave rain, and the earth
produced its fruit.
(James 5:16–18)

Whatever things you ask in
prayer, believing, you will receive.
(Matt. 21:22)

You do not have because you do
not ask. (James 4:2)

[Jesus said,] "Whatever you ask
the Father in My name He will
give you . . . Ask, and you will
receive, that your joy may be full."
(John 16:23–24)

What wonderful gifts God has given to us! To each person,
He has given a desire to succeed—in other words, He has given
us the *motivation* we need to pursue success. He has given us
talents and abilities—when we develop them and use them for
His purposes, we can be assured of success. He has given us
the Holy Spirit to strengthen us in our areas of weakness and
to give us daily counsel into the right choices and decisions we
should make in order to become successful. And He has given
us the privilege of prayer so that we might activate our faith
and use it to bring about the character and courage He desires
for us to have.

God not only wants us to know *how* to be successful in the-
ory. He has given us all we need to be successful in reality.

• *What new insights do you have into God's desire for you to be successful?*

_____

_____

• *How do you feel about God's commitment to your success?*

_____

_____

THREE

SETTING GODLY GOALS

One of the most important questions you can ever ask is, "What goals does *God* desire for me to set and to achieve, and in the process, to be a success in His eyes?" Setting *God's* goals for your life is a critical step toward being a success in God's eyes.

One of the most goal-oriented people in the Bible is the apostle Paul. In writing to the Philippians, Paul said,

> But what things were gain to me, these I have counted loss for Christ. Yet indeed I also count all things loss for the excellence of the knowledge of Christ Jesus my Lord, for whom I have suffered the loss of all things, and count them as rubbish, that I may gain Christ and be found in Him . . . that I may know Him and the power of His resurrection, and the fellowship of His sufferings, being conformed to His death, if, by any means, I may attain to the resurrection from the dead. Not that I have already attained, or am already perfected; but I press on, that I may lay hold of that for which Christ Jesus has also laid hold of me. Brethren, I do not count myself to have apprehended; but one thing I do, forgetting those things which are behind and reaching forward to those things which are ahead, I press toward the goal for the prize of the upward call of God in Christ Jesus. (Phil. 3:7–14)

Paul was not a man who wasted time or energy. He was extremely focused in his life, and he had an overwhelming sense of purpose and direction. He clearly stated his life goals to the Philippians:

- to know Christ Jesus as intimately as possible,
- to experience the righteousness of Christ in his own life, and
- to be conformed to Christ in every way.

We know from the descriptions of Paul's ministry in the book of Acts that he also had another goal: to reach as many people as possible with the message of Jesus Christ's crucifixion and resurrection, and to do so with a sense of urgency.

• *What new insights do you have into the above passage from Philippians 3?*

_____

_____

Paul made no claim that he had achieved his life goals. Rather, he stated that he was continuing to *press* toward the goal of the prize of the "upward call of God in Christ Jesus." *To press*, in this case, means "to diligently follow after." Paul was zealous in following Christ.

• *In your life, have you identified your main life goal? Is it a desire to be fully conformed to Christ Jesus?*

_____

_____

What Are Godly Goals?

A goal is an aim, a purpose, a sense of direction toward which a person moves all of his energies, desires, and efforts. Goals are the "targets" toward which we point our lives.

A goal involves an organized, planned "stretching" of your life. If you have already achieved something, it is no longer a goal—it is an accomplishment. A goal is a statement of intention, aimed at the future. It is a statement of how you desire to grow, develop, mature, or change in a positive, specific, and achievable way.

Every Christian is called to set "knowing and serving Christ" as his primary life goal. All other goals are to be placed under this broad umbrella goal.

Goals for the Christian are not based upon how we desire to live for our own pleasure and satisfaction. Rather, we live as unto the Lord. We are *His* possession, bought with a price— the precious blood of Jesus Christ. We belong to God, and our goals must be ones that bring pleasure to Him.

What the Word Says	What the Word Says to Me
Or do you not know that your body is the temple of the Holy Spirit who is in you, whom you have from God, and you are not your own? For you were bought at a price; therefore glorify God in your body and in your spirit, which are God's. (1 Cor. 6:19–20)	-------------------------------
I have been crucified with Christ; it is no longer I who live, but Christ lives in me; and the life which I now live in the flesh I live by faith in the Son of God, who loved me and gave Himself for me. (Gal. 2:20)	-------------------------------
Walk in love, as Christ also has loved us and given Himself for	-------------------------------

us, an offering and a sacrifice to
God for a sweet-smelling aroma.
(Eph. 5:2)

I beseech you therefore,
brethren, by the mercies of God,
that you present your bodies a
living sacrifice, holy, acceptable
to God, which is your reasonable
service. And do not be conformed to this world, but be
transformed by the renewing
of your mind, that you may
prove what is that good and
acceptable and perfect will of
God. (Rom. 12:1–2)

For whom He foreknew, He also
predestined to be conformed to
the image of His Son, that He
might be the firstborn among
many brethren. Moreover whom
He predestined, these He also
called; whom He called, these
He also justified; and whom He
justified, these He also glorified.
(Rom. 8:29–30)

I have found it very helpful in my life to identify and to write
down my priority goal. It is this: "To know Christ as intimately
and fully as possible." My secondary goal, which sets the pattern for my life and determines the details of my daily
schedule, is this: "To get the gospel of Jesus Christ to as many
people as possible, as clearly as possible, as quickly as possible, as irresistibly as possible, by the power of the Holy Spirit
and to the glory of God." Period. That's *why* I live.

I encourage you to reflect upon your priority goal in life, and to state your priority goal and your secondary goals in writing.

> • *In your life, have you identified a "priority goal"? Can you state it in concise terms?*

_____

_____

> • *In your life, have you identified your secondary goals?*

_____

_____

Goals help a person maintain focus. They help a person avoid stray topics, relationships, and activities that can become distractions and sometimes deterrents. They help a person set his schedule, not only over long periods of time, but daily. Goals help put life in balance. Take a look at the chart below and consider your own life:

Person with No Goals	**Person with Goals**
Adrift	Sense of direction
No excitement in living	Excitement in living
Accepts mediocrity	Pursues excellence
Critical of others who are successful	Appreciates others who are successsful
Disappointed with life	Strong sense of purpose, value, and worth
Settles for living in a rut	Seeks a creative, active life
Bad steward of God's gifts of time, energy, resources	Seeks a balanced life marked by emotional and physical health

> • *How do you feel about your own life? Which type of person do you desire to be?*

_____

_____

Should Christians Set Goals for the Future?

There are those in the body of Christ who contend that Christians should not set goals. I want to take a look at two main passages of Scripture that critics of goal-setting often use to support their belief.

The Case for Contentment

The first passage often used to teach that goal-setting is not biblical is Hebrews 13:5, which says,

> Let your conduct be without covetousness; be content with such things as you have. For He Himself has said, "I will never leave you nor forsake you."

To be content, in the context of this verse, is in direct relationship to the statement, "Let your conduct be without covetousness." We are never to covet what others have. Contentment is realizing that God is the Source of *all that we need for our present happiness*. It is being thankful for what the Lord is providing, even as we plan for our future. It is trusting that the Lord will never leave us nor forsake us. It is experiencing the peace of God *in the midst of any circumstance or situation*, even as we make our requests known to God.

Contentment is not settling for a settled-down life. Rather, it is a feeling of being at "rest" in our relationship with the Lord, even as we pursue greater wholeness and prosperity.

What the Word Says	What the Word Says to Me
Not that I speak in regard to need, for I have learned in whatever state I am, to be content. (Phil. 4:11)	
You shall not covet your neighbor's house; you shall not	

covet your neighbor's wife,
nor his male servant, nor his
female servant, nor his ox, nor
his donkey, nor anything that is
your neighbor's. (Ex. 20:17)

Be anxious for nothing, but in
everything by prayer and supplication, with thanksgiving, let
your requests be made known
to God; and the peace of God,
which surpasses all understanding, will guard your
hearts and minds through
Christ Jesus. (Phil. 4:6–7)

•*What new insights do you have into the relationship between contentment and success?*

_____

_____

Living Each Day As It Comes

Matthew 6:31–34 is another passage that is often used to counteract a need for goal-setting:

[Jesus taught,] "Therefore do not worry, saying, 'What shall we eat?' or 'What shall we drink?' or 'What shall we wear?' For after all these things the Gentiles seek. For your heavenly Father knows that you need all these things. But seek first the kingdom of God and His righteousness, and all these things shall be added to you. Therefore do not worry about tomorrow, for tomorrow will worry about its own things. Sufficient for the day is its own trouble."

This passage has nothing to do with planning or not planning. Rather, it is about feeling anxious about whether God will provide our day-to-day needs for food, shelter, and clothing.

This is also a great statement about our priorities. Note that Jesus says we are to seek *first* the kingdom of God and His righteousness. Seeking the kingdom of God and His righteousness is a *goal*. It is the foremost thing worth pursuing and worth establishing in one's life.

Seeking the kingdom of God and His righteousness does not happen automatically. It happens because we set our minds and hearts toward those things that build our inner character and that yield eternal reward.

What the Word Says	What the Word Says to Me
Seek those things which are above, where Christ is, sitting at the right hand of God. Set your mind on things above, not on things on the earth. (Col. 3:1–2)	....
Pursue righteousness, godliness, faith, love, patience, gentleness. Fight the good fight of faith, lay hold on eternal life, to which you were also called and have confessed. (1 Tim. 6:11–12)	....

Four Questions to Ask About the Goals You Set

As you set any goal in your life, ask yourself these four questions:

1. *Why, Lord, is this important to You?* If you understand the answer to why a goal is important to the Lord,

you'll be in a good position to seek answers to other questions: How? When? Where? With whom?

2. *Lord, does this fit into Your plan for my life?* Some tasks may be good, but not be God's best for you. Ask the Lord what fits you best, given your talents, abilities, and skills.

3. *Is this goal totally in line with God's Word?* God will not lead you to pursue a goal that is contrary to the principles established in the Bible.

4. *How might the accomplishment of this goal bring blessing to others?* God gives us goals so He might do two things simultaneously—He desires to perform a refining work in our own lives, and, at the same time, to perform a work that will benefit others and be for their eternal good.

• *In your life, which of your goals do NOT meet this four-fold criteria? Which ones do?*

_____

_____

What the Word Says	**What the Word Says to Me**
[Jesus said,] "Ask, and it will be given to you; seek, and you will find; knock, and it will be opened to you. For everyone who asks receives, and he who seeks finds, and to him who knocks it will be opened." (Matt. 7:7–8)	---------------------------- ---------------------------- ---------------------------- ---------------------------- ---------------------------- ---------------------------- ---------------------------- ----------------------------

Writing Down Your Goals

It is important that you write down your goals. The Lord spoke to Jeremiah: "Write in a book for yourself all the words that I have spoken to you" (Jer. 30:2; see also Jer. 36:2). The Lord said to the prophet Habakkuk,

> Write the vision
> And make it plain on tablets,
> That he may run who reads it. (Hab. 2:2)

Put a Date with a Goal

Some goals are lifelong, but even lifelong goals can be broken down into smaller goals that can be accomplished in short- and medium-range time periods. Identify your goals that are

- *immediate*—things to be done each day, or that can be accomplished in a week or month;
- *short-range*—those goals that may take one to three months or even as long as a year; and
- *long-range*—those goals that may extend beyond a year.

Consider All Areas of Your Life

Goals can be set in each of life's main areas:

1. Spiritual
2. Personal
3. Family
4. Vocation
5. Social
6. Financial

Take a look at the goals that you believe are God's plan for you. Do you have goals in each of these areas? Do your goals tend to cluster mainly in one or two areas? If you are neglecting certain areas of your life, or are placing too much emphasis on one or two areas, your life is not truly balanced. Seek to establish wholeness.

• *In your life, are you setting and seeking to accomplish goals in each area of your life?*

_____

_____

Be Specific

State precisely what you intend to accomplish—avoid fuzzy generalities. When Jesus met Bartimaeus at the outskirts of Jericho, He asked Bartimaeus one simple question: "What do you want Me to do for you?" (Mark 10:51). Jesus could see that Bartimaeus was blind, yet Jesus asked Bartimaeus this question so that *Bartimaeus* might confront his need and face fully the prospect of his own healing. Do you truly *want* the specifics of the goals you have written down? Why do you want to accomplish what you have stated as goals? What are your motives? Do you truly want to *live* the way you would live if your goals were accomplished?

Set Goals You Cannot Reach on Your Own Strength and Ability

A truly God-given goal always has a "faith factor" to it. It is a goal that will stretch you, challenge you, cause you to grow in spirit, and that will cause you to rely on God for help, wisdom, strength, and results.

What the Word Says	What the Word Says to Me
When I say to the righteous that he shall surely live, but he trusts in his own righteousness and commits iniquity, none of his righteous works shall be remembered. (Ezek. 33:13)	_____ _____ _____ _____ _____ _____
Behold, God is my salvation, I will trust and not be afraid;	_____ _____

"For Yah, the LORD, is my
strength and song;
He also has become
my salvation."
(Isa. 12:2)

For I will not trust in my bow,
Nor shall my sword save me.
In God we boast all day long.
(Ps. 44:6, 8)

Take one step at a time as you establish your goals. Wait upon the Lord for His direction and guidance. Test your goals against the Scriptures and see if they endure over time. Few things worth attaining can be accomplished in a day. What matters most is our slow, steadfast, obedient pursuit of those goals to which God calls us. He is as concerned about our ongoing faithfulness, discipline, faith, obedience, and reliance upon Him as He is about our accomplishing the goals He helps us establish.

- *What new insights do you have into the relationship between goals and godly success?*

- *How do you feel about the goals you have set for your life?*

- *In what ways are you being challenged to set new goals or revise old ones?*

FOUR

GOD'S PERSONAL SUCCESS PATTERN FOR YOU

O ne of the greatest differences between the world's message about success and God's plan for success is this: The world seeks one formula that produces one set of results for all people. God's plan is far more creative, far more individualized, and far more personal. His *principles* don't change. But God's formula for success always takes into account *your* unique set of spiritual gifts, natural talents, personality, circumstances, and situations.

In this study, we are going to take a look at the lives of three men who portrayed distinctly different patterns of success.

God's Pattern of Success for Joseph

Joseph, the eleventh of twelve sons born to Jacob, was a man who had an understanding of God's personal "success plan" for his life in his youth. He was given divine insight into God's plan for his future, which included great prominence, power, and prestige. His understanding of his personal future success was based upon two dreams God gave to him when he was only seventeen years old. (You can read about these dreams in Genesis 37:5–9.)

Like many people today, Joseph had a dream of success, but no *plan* for success. God had given him a glimpse of his future but had not provided the intervening details. It was up to Joseph to pursue God's plan for success with faith and obedience in doing the things the Lord put in his path to do.

> • *In reflecting back over your life, was there a "dream" that God planted in your heart when you were a young person about what you would be and do in your future?*

_____

_____

God never asks any of us to sit down and wait idly for Him to vault us into success. He asks us to trust and obey Him day by day, day in and day out, and to learn the lessons He sets before us. Some of the work that God gives us to do may seem menial and totally unrelated to the end result of our success. What we often do not perceive is that God is building a strong pattern of experience, skill, trustworthiness, honesty, integrity, and character into us, so that when the time comes for us to be in a position of authority or influence, we will be ready.

The success we achieve is never of our own doing. God's hand is always in both the process and the results. Joseph knew this. And when he finally did persevere with faith in God through abandonment by his brothers, slavery in a foreign land, false accusations, and imprisonment, he was prepared to exercise authority with wisdom. Not only did Joseph make wise decisions, but he gave God the glory for bringing him to a position in which he could help his family and countless others. He said to his brothers later in his life,

> God sent me before you to preserve a posterity for you in the earth, and to save your lives by a great deliverance. So now it was not you who sent me here, but God; and He has made me a father to Pharaoh, and lord of all his house, and a ruler throughout all the land of Egypt. (Gen. 45:7–8)

• *In reflecting back over your life, can you see how the Lord has used various experiences to teach you trust and obedience? Can you cite specific instances that He has used to build your character and integrity?*

_____

_____

The success plan for Joseph's life might be summarized like this:

Vision
followed by years of
faithful preparation, trust, and obedience
resulting in years of
service, authority, and reward

• *Is this the pattern for success that the Lord seems to be implementing in your life or in the life of someone you know? At which stage are you presently? How do you feel about this pattern for success?*

_____

_____

What the Word Says

You meant evil against me; but God meant it for good, in order to bring it about as it is this day, to save many people alive. (Gen. 50:20)

We know that all things work together for good to those who love God, to those who are the called according to His purpose. (Rom. 8:28)

What the Word Says to Me

[The apostle Paul said,] "I was
not disobedient to the heavenly
vision." (Acts 26:19)

[The Lord said through Isaiah,]
"I am God, and there is no
other;
I am God, and there
is none like Me. . .
My counsel shall stand,
And I will do all My pleasure. . .
I will also bring it to pass.
I have purposed it;
I will also do it." (Isa. 46:9–11)

God's Pattern of Success for Moses

The pattern for success that we see in Moses' life is very different from that of Joseph. Moses did not have a vision for success early in his life, although he experienced a certain degree of privilege as an adopted son of Pharaoh. He grew up separated from his people. After murdering an Egyptian, he ran for his life to the remote desert region of Midian, and there he married and spent nearly forty years tending sheep.

Then the day came when the Lord revealed Himself to Moses and gave him a specific mission for his life.

Many people today grow up knowing "about" the Lord but not knowing the Lord personally. They go through difficult and sometimes devastating experiences in their lives, and then one day, they come face-to-face with the reality of God and the reality of their own lives. Moses argued with God about his worthiness to pursue the goals God set before him. He eventually relented and went to Pharaoh with the message from God, "Let My people go."

For forty years, Moses led the Israelites out of Egypt, across the wilderness, to the promised land. The success pattern that the Lord seemed to have for him was this:

Seemingly unrelated events
without the person having a vision of success followed by a
definite and specific call of God
followed by
faithful obedience and trust

• *Is this the pattern of success that God seems to be implementing in your life or in the life of someone you know? Where are you in this process? How do you feel about God's success pattern for you?*

_____

_____

A similar pattern might be seen in the life of the apostle Paul. Paul grew up studying God's Law and being the best Pharisee and Roman citizen he could possibly be. Then came his experience on the Damascus Road in which he surrendered his life to Christ. Suddenly Paul's life began to make sense. He could see ways in which he had been perfectly prepared for the plan God had for him. He knew the Scriptures so he could explain with depth and clarity how Christ Jesus fulfilled them. He had the freedom to travel and speak freely throughout the Roman empire. He knew the Jews and their customs and had access to their synagogues. He also knew that God could redeem even the most hardened sinful heart, and therefore, he was quick to extend the mercy of God to the Gentiles.

• *In reflecting back over your life, can you see ways in which the Lord has "built into you" the abilities, skills, and readiness to take on the challenges He is now presenting to you?*

_____

_____

What the Word Says

For I know the thoughts that I think toward you, says the LORD, thoughts of peace and not of

What the Word Says to Me

----

evil, to give you a future and
a hope. (Jer. 29:11)

[Jesus said,] "But when the
Helper comes, whom I shall
send to you from the Father,
the Spirit of truth who proceeds
from the Father, He will testify
of Me. And you also will bear
witness." (John 15:26–27)

Show me Your ways, O LORD;
Teach me Your paths.
Lead me in Your truth
and teach me,
For You are the God
of my salvation;
On You I wait all the day.
(Ps. 25:4–5)

God's Pattern of Success for David

There is a third pattern of success we see in the life of King David. He was a man who came to a knowledge of the Lord as a youngster, was anointed by God for a great future as a teenager, and experienced a series of visible and outward successes throughout his life, one building upon another.

This does not mean that David did not encounter difficult times. These situations, however, were ones that *strengthened* David and further prepared him for greater things ahead. How was it that David was not defeated by jealousy, exile, warring enemies, traitorous followers, rebellious children, or even his own sinfulness? He was not defeated because in each instance, David *turned to the Lord in repentance and in trust.* Any detours or mistakes were quickly reversed through David's repentant heart, his humility before the Lord, and his desire to serve God fully. David never stopped acknowledging God as the Source of his strength.

The pattern of David's success might be described this way:

Anointing by God
followed by
success built upon success

• *Is this the pattern of success that the Lord seems to be implementing in your life or in the life of someone you know?*

_____

_____

The apostle Peter seems to have experienced a similar pattern for success in his life. Peter was a successful fisherman when Jesus first met him, and he continued to enjoy a great deal of success as he followed Jesus. He was one of Jesus' inner circle, along with James and John, and he was the apostle to whom Jesus spoke the most.

Peter certainly had failures and made mistakes. He rebuked Jesus when Jesus spoke of His crucifixion, he failed in his faith when it came to calming a storm, he relied on his own strength when he cut off the ear of a high priest's servant, and he denied Jesus three times after Jesus' arrest. But these were all incidents of which Peter quickly repented.

After the resurrection of Jesus, it was Peter who became the leader of the church. It was Peter who preached a sermon on the Day of Pentecost that resulted in three thousand members being added to the newly established church. It was Peter who brought healing to the lame man at the Beautiful Gate, who raised a paralyzed man from his bed, and who raised Dorcas from the dead—all in the name of Jesus. It was Peter who opened the door to the Gentiles, defended the rights of the Gentile Christians, and who established the earliest believers in the "way" of Jesus.

Many Christians today are raised in godly homes, and they come to know the Lord early in their lives. Then the Lord seems to direct them into a very specific avenue of ministry or service. They continue to grow and mature, becoming increasingly conformed to Christ. Their effectiveness as witnesses to Christ also continues to grow. Their life pattern is one that reflects a pattern of moving from strength to strength.

What the Word Says	**What the Word Says to Me**
The LORD is my light and my salvation. . . The LORD is the strength of my life. (Ps. 27:1)	_____ _____ _____ _____
The hope of the righteous will be gladness. . . The way of the LORD is strength for the upright. (Prov. 10:28–29)	_____ _____ _____ _____ _____
For whom He foreknew, He also predestined to be conformed to the image of His Son, that He might be the firstborn among many brethren. Moreover whom He predestined, these He also called; whom He called, these He also justified; and whom He justified, these He also glorified. (Rom. 8:29–30)	_____ _____ _____ _____ _____ _____ _____ _____ _____
He who walks righteously and speaks uprightly, He who despises the gain of oppressions, Who gestures with his hands, refusing bribes, Who stops his ears from hearing of bloodshed, And shuts his eyes from seeing evil:	_____ _____ _____ _____ _____ _____ _____ _____

He will dwell on high;
His place of defense will
be the fortress of rocks;
Bread will be given him,
His water will be sure.
(Isa. 33:15–16)

A Unique Pattern for Each Person

Was Joseph more successful than Moses? Was King David more successful than Joseph? No! Each was successful in his own life *according to the pattern that God had established for him.*

God does not deal with any one of us exactly as He deals or has dealt with another person. Even if God seems to be implementing one of the three patterns described in this lesson, the exact circumstances and situations that He allows in our lives and the call to which He calls us is unique.

Never covet another person's success. Never discount what the Lord is doing in your life. To do so is to greatly hinder the work that God desires to do in you and stall the fulfillment of God's success plan for your life.

• *What new insights do you have into the way God works in a life to bring about success?*

• *How do you feel about the success that may still lie ahead for you?*

• *In reflecting back over your life, are there specific ways in which you are feeling challenged to take a "next step" in pursuing the goals God has led you to establish? Are there specific things of which you need to repent or specific changes you need to make in your life?*

FIVE

PURSUING GOD'S GOALS

If I were to draw a line in front of you today and I said, "Step over this line, and your life will be better, beginning today," would you step over that line? I feel certain you would! I give you that challenge today regarding the pursuit of your own goals because it is not enough for a person to set goals or to recognize the ways in which God is working in their life. We each must make a decision to *pursue* God's goals and to pursue them *God's way*.

Doing Things God's Way

God not only deals in terms of what and who, but He also deals in "how." How we reach our goals is critical to our being successful, not only in attaining the goals God helps us set, but in developing the character that God wants us to have. The principles for *how* to reach our God-given goals can be found in the story of David and Goliath.

Let me give you a little background. The army of the Philistines was encamped on one side of a valley, and the army of Israel was on the other side. For forty consecutive days, the "champion" of the Philistines—Goliath, their number-one warrior—had come out and stood in front of his army and shouted to the Israelites, "I defy the armies of Israel this day; give me a man, that we may fight together" (1 Sam. 17:10).

Goliath and the Philistines set the terms for the battle. They wanted the contest to be one man versus one man, with the outcome being that if the Philistine won, all the Israelites would become their servants. A great deal was at stake.

Day after day, the Israelites failed to respond to Goliath's challenge.

Many of us find ourselves in the same position when it comes to the pursuit of our goals. We see a giant obstacle standing between where we are at present and where we want to be. That obstacle fills us with fear; it holds out the prospect of defeat and loss. We fail to act.

> • *In your life, can you cite instances in which fear kept you from pursuing godly goals?*

_____

_____

Ten Aspects of Pursuing a Goal God's Way

David arrived on the scene and was angered by what he heard and saw. He immediately established a goal that he believed with his whole heart was a goal that God desired for him to accomplish. There are ten important aspects of David's goal setting:

1. A Clear Picture of the Goal and Its Rewards

Upon hearing Goliath's challenge, David asked, "What shall be done for the man who kills this Philistine and takes away the reproach from Israel? For who is this uncircumcised Philistine, that he should defy the armies of the living God?" (1 Sam. 17:26).

David's statement is firmly rooted in his belief that Goliath needed to be defeated, could be defeated, and *would* be defeated. He saw the killing of Goliath as an achievable goal and certainly one that must have rewards associated with it.

At this time, David had already been anointed to be the next king of Israel, although only David and the prophet Samuel knew about his anointing. For David, the victory over Goliath was not a personal act of bravery as much as it was an act of a future king on behalf of his people. David fully expected to be successful in his pursuit of God's goals for his life, and he expected to rule a people who were free of the Philistines, not slaves to them.

> • *In your life, are your goals clear and concise? Are they relevant to God's greater purposes for your life? Do they impact the "big picture" of your future in Christ Jesus?*

_____

_____

2. A Consuming Desire to Reach the Goal

David could not be talked out of pursuing his goal. His brothers tried to dissuade him, but David refused to leave, refused to be discouraged, and refused to quit talking about Goliath's defeat.

If your goals are truly from the Lord, you will have a feeling deep within you that you *must* accomplish them in order to be obedient to the Lord and to bring benefit to others.

What the Word Says	What the Word Says to Me
[The prophet Jeremiah said of God's call on his life,] "His word was in my heart like a burning fire Shut up in my bones; I was weary of holding it back, And I could not." (Jer. 20:9)	------------------------------- ------------------------------- ------------------------------- ------------------------------- ------------------------------- ------------------------------- -------------------------------
Be kindly affectionate to one another with brotherly love . . . not lagging in diligence, fervent	------------------------------- ------------------------------- -------------------------------

in spirit, serving the Lord.
(Rom. 12:10–11)

It is good to be zealous in a
good thing always. (Gal. 4:18)

> • *Is the Lord challenging you today with something that is burning inside you—a goal that you MUST pursue?*

---

3. Confidence in the Lord's Help

David had no doubt whatsoever that with the Lord's help, he would be able to kill Goliath. He boldly said to King Saul, "Let no man's heart fail because of him; your servant will go and fight with this Philistine" (1 Sam. 17:32). David wasn't confident in his own ability. He said about his victory over a lion and bear while tending sheep, and about his upcoming victory over Goliath, "The LORD . . . will deliver me from the hand of this Philistine" (vs. 37).

David rushed down the mountainside toward Goliath crying, "This day the LORD will deliver you into my hand . . . that all the earth may know that there is a God in Israel. Then all this assembly shall know that the LORD does not save with sword and spear; for the battle is the LORD's, and He will give you into our hands" (1 Sam. 17:46–47).

> • *How do you feel as you read these words of David? How do you feel today about the Lord helping you to achieve your godly goals?*

What the Word Says	**What the Word Says to Me**
I can do all things through Christ who strengthens me. (Phil. 4:13)	--

The Lord is faithful, who will
establish you and guard you
from the evil one. And we have
confidence in the Lord con-
cerning you. (2 Thess. 3:3–4)

The LORD will be your
confidence,
And will keep your foot from
being caught. (Prov. 3:26)

------

4. A Course for Action

David didn't go into battle without first getting Saul's approval. He went through the right "channels" (see 1 Sam. 17:37). David then chose the right armor, or the right "method," for the upcoming battle he faced. He went into battle with weapons that were right for his unique talents, abilities, experience, and skills.

Too often we try to accomplish our goals using man-made methods that may work for another person, but which are totally unsuited to our abilities and talents. Trust God to reveal to you *His* method for pursuing *your* success.

What the Word Says   **What the Word Says to Me**

Teach me to do Your will,
For You are my God;
Your Spirit is good.
Lead me in the land of
uprightness. (Ps. 143:10)

Happy is the man
who finds wisdom,
And the man who
gains understanding.
Her ways are ways of pleasantness,

And all her paths are peace.	--
(Prov. 3:13, 17)	--
It is God who arms me with	--
strength,	--
And makes my way perfect.	--
He makes my feet like the feet	--
of deer,	--
And sets me on my high	--
places. (Ps. 18:32–33)	--

5. No Delay in Pursuing an Immediate Goal

David did not procrastinate, make excuses, or stall. He took action.

> • *In your life, have you "delayed" in pursuing goals that you felt were immediate? What was the result?*

_____

_____

6. Cooperation

David sought and relied on the cooperation of others. The battle against the Philistines was not a one-man show. David may have fought Goliath one-on-one, but he did not take on the entire Philistine army single-handedly. Prior to facing Goliath, David had spread his own confidence throughout the Israelite camp. The soldiers were stirred up, ready to take on the battle as soon as David was victorious. The moment David cut off Goliath's head, "the men of Israel and Judah arose and shouted, and pursued the Philistines as far as the entrance to the valley and to the gates of Ekron" (1 Sam. 17:52).

If the Lord has laid a goal on your heart, He is already working to prepare the hearts of others to help you reach your goal. Or, He may be working in you to help another person with a goal you share. Either way, we ultimately are to work together to spread the gospel, extend the kingdom of God, and build up the body of Christ.

Seek out those with whom you can work toward a common goal.

7. Consistency in Pursuing the Goal

David did not lose sight of the big goal of his life, which was to serve God as king of Israel. After defeating Goliath, he took the head of Goliath back to Jerusalem as a signal to all the people that the Lord had delivered them from their enemy. He also took the armor of Goliath into his own tent as a constant reminder of what the Lord had enabled him to do. David knew that in the years ahead, he would *need* to be reminded that God was bigger than any problem he faced. He knew that the Israelites needed to be *encouraged* to trust the Lord more.

Don't lose sight of your long-range goals, even as you throw your energies into accomplishing your short-term or immediate goals.

Paul encouraged Titus that believers are to "maintain good works" even as they "meet urgent needs"—to get caught up in urgent needs and to fail to maintain the overall good work of our life is to be "unfruitful" (see Titus 3:14).

What the Word Says	What the Word Says to Me
You shall walk in all the ways which the LORD your God has commanded you, that you may live and that it may be well with you, and that you may prolong your days in the land which you shall possess. (Deut. 5:33)	--
Beware lest you also fall from your own steadfastness, being led away with the error of the wicked; but grow in the grace and knowledge of our Lord and Savior Jesus Christ. (2 Peter 3:17–18)	--

8. Emotions Kept Under Control

David could have become frustrated or angry at the opposition his brothers gave him. He could have become embroiled in arguments with the other soldiers. He could have become discouraged and gone back home. David didn't give in to any of these options. He saved all of his emotional energy for the battle.

As you pursue your God-given goals, make a decision to save your emotional energy for those moments, decisions, and actions that are truly *important* for you to reach your goal. There are many things that can, and must, be overlooked or not blown out of proportion.

Keep your focus on God's love, God's call, God's help, God's approval, and God's rewards. He will not disappoint you or fail you, if you continue to pursue the goals He sets for your life with focus and determination.

> • *As you reflect back over your life, are there experiences you have had in which you allowed emotions to get out of control, with the end result being that you were deterred or "detoured" away from your major goals?*

_____

_____

As we pursue our goals, we each will face situations that can cause us to experience fear. Take charge over fear! Encourage yourself in the Lord. Choose to encourage others around you and to associate with upbeat, faith-filled people who can encourage you daily.

Later in David's life, he faced a defeat. Amalekites entered David's stronghold at Ziklag while David and his men were out of the city, and they set fire to the city and took captive all of the women and children. We read in 1 Samuel 30:6, "Now David was greatly distressed, for the people spoke of stoning him, because the soul of all the people was grieved, every man for his sons and his daughters. But David strengthened himself in the LORD his God."

David encouraged himself in the Lord. He focused on what God was able to do rather than on what man had done. He asked the Lord if he should pursue the troops that had done evil to him and his men, and the Lord said, "Pursue." So David and four hundred of his men went in pursuit, and "David recovered all that the Amalekites had carried away" (vs. 18). I encourage you to read this entire story in 1 Samuel 30.

> • *What new insights do you have into 1 Samuel 30 and into the ways in which the Lord may be calling you to encourage yourself in Him after a setback or defeat?*

---

9. Courage Developed Over Time

David had courage that had been developed over years and through a variety of experiences. David did not suddenly awaken one morning and have courage to confront Goliath. He had developed courage as a shepherd boy, protecting his father's flocks against the elements and against predatory animals, including a lion and a bear. David no doubt had experienced many moments in which he'd had to stare down his own fears while alone with his flocks in wilderness areas.

Ask the Lord today to give you the *daily* courage you need as you face the tasks and temptations before you. Ask Him to give you courage to accomplish the immediate and short-range goals you have set. That will be your best possible means of developing the courage you will need when major crises or obstacles arise.

What the Word Says	What the Word Says to Me
Behave courageously, and the LORD will be with the good. (2 Chron. 19:11)	

Wait on the LORD;
Be of good courage,
And He shall strengthen
your heart;
Wait, I say, on the LORD!
(Ps. 27:14)

For God has not given us a
spirit of fear, but of power and
of love and of a sound mind.
(2 Tim. 1:7)

10. A Conscious Dependence on God at All Times

Throughout the story of David's battle with Goliath we find references to the Lord. David had a conscious, openly expressed dependence on God.

Let your conversations and your statements to others reflect your dependence upon the Lord. Remember at all times that none of us can accomplish anything of eternal benefit in our own strength.

> • *What new insights do you have into the WAY in which God desires for you to pursue the goals He has laid on your heart?*

> • *How do you feel today as you look at the goals you have set? What "course of action" do you believe is best for you to take immediately?*

> • *In what ways are you feeling challenged in your spirit regarding the way you have pursued, are pursuing, and intend to pursue your God-given goals?*

SIX

MONEY AND SUCCESS

One of the greatest deceptions in our nation today is that success equals wealth. Becoming the person God wants you to be and achieving the goals He sets for your life are what make a person genuinely successful.

Wealth has virtually nothing to do with your *becoming* the person God wants you to be. And wealth, solely for the sake of acquiring wealth, is not a goal that God sets for a person's life. You will find no admonition of God in the Bible for a person to seek and strive to become rich materially.

Does this mean a rich person cannot be successful in God's eyes? Does it mean that God never blesses a person with material wealth or nice possessions? No. It means that wealth is not the gauge by which we are to determine success. God has different standards of measurement.

In this lesson, we are going to take a look at what the Bible says about money. (If this topic is of special interest to you, I encourage you to read the study guide in this series titled *Understanding Financial Stewardship.*)

What the Bible Teaches About Money

The Bible has more verses devoted to finances and money, and our proper use of them, than to verses about heaven! God knew money was a practical matter that would require our attention on a daily basis. Money is a vital part of our lives.

For the most part, the Bible regards money as simply a medium of exchange. It is intended to be used for good and righteous purposes. It is a blessing of God given to us so that we might be stewards of a portion of the Lord's bountiful supply. In many cases, it is a tool that God uses to test our trust and faithfulness. The apostle Paul taught,

> We urge you, brethren, that you increase more and more; that you also aspire to lead a quiet life, to mind your own business, and to work with your own hands, as we commanded you, that you may walk properly toward those who are outside, and that you may lack nothing. (1 Thess. 4:10–12)

These verses have a two-fold message:

First, the Lord expects us to *work* so we are *not* in financial or material need.

Second, the Lord desires for us to *increase more and more.*

•*What new insights do you have into 1 Thessalonians 4:10–12?*

_____

_____

• *How do you feel as you read this passage of Scripture?*

_____

_____

Three Key Principles

The Bible has three overriding principles regarding money and material wealth. We are wise to keep them in mind always.

1. God Is the Source of All Blessings

All wealth comes from God. Anytime we look at what we have in terms of possessions or financial holdings, we should be quick to say, "God is the One who has given me this."

• *In your experience, what tends to be your first response when you receive a raise, promotion, or unexpected financial windfall? Is your first response to thank and praise God, or is it to feel self-satisfaction at what you have accomplished?*

_____

_____

2. There Is No Lasting Ownership of Anything Material

Even those things that you believe you have bought and paid for are not things that you will own forever. None of us can take any material blessing from this life into eternity.

• *In your experience, can you recall a time when you "lost" something—property, a possession, an heirloom, an inheritance—that you had thought would be yours for your entire life?*

_____

_____

3. We Are Privileged by God to Use Things to Bless People

God allows certain amounts of wealth and certain possessions to come into our hands so that we might use them to bring blessing to others. We are to be a "funnel" for God's blessings, not a container in which to hoard them. We must always be determined to use things and love people, rather than love things and use people!

What the Word Says	What the Word Says to Me
As for every man to whom God has given riches and wealth, and given him power to eat of it, to receive his heritage and rejoice in his labor—this is the gift of God. (Eccl. 5:19)	....
	....
	....
	....
	....
	....

Beware that you do not forget
the LORD your God by not keeping His commandments . . .
lest—when you have eaten and
are full, and have built beautiful
houses and dwell in them . . .
you say in your heart, "My
power and the might of my hand
have gained me this wealth."
And you shall remember the
LORD your God, for it is He who
gives you power to get wealth,
that He may establish His
covenant which He swore
to your fathers, as it is this day.
(Deut. 8:11–12, 17–18)

Five Things Jesus Taught About Money

Many people conclude that Jesus favored poverty and had very little good to say about wealth. Let's take a closer look at five things Jesus taught about money.

1. The Pursuit of Wealth Must Never Be Our Number-One Priority

Jesus gave us this very solemn warning about a love for money: "For what profit is it to a man if he gains the whole world, and loses his own soul? Or what will a man give in exchange for his soul?" (Matt. 16:26). Jesus plainly taught that we are to seek first the kingdom of God and that those who make the acquisition of wealth their top priority will find it very difficult to gain heavenly reward.

What the Word Says	What the Word Says to Me
[Jesus taught,] "Assuredly, I say to you that it is hard for a rich	

man to enter the kingdom of
heaven. And again I say to you,
it is easier for a camel to go
through the eye of a needle than
for a rich man to enter the kingdom of God." (Matt. 19:23–24)

[Jesus said,] "Seek first the
kingdom of God and His
righteousness, and all these
things shall be added to you."
(Matt. 6:33)

[Jesus taught,] "Do not lay up
for yourselves treasures on earth,
where moth and rust destroy
and where thieves break in and
steal; but lay up for yourselves
treasures in heaven, where neither moth nor rust destroys
and where thieves do not break
in and steal. For where your
treasure is, there your heart will
be also." (Matt. 6:19–21)

2. We Err Greatly When We Hoard Our Wealth and Fail to Give Generously to Those in Need

One day a man came to Jesus and said, "Teacher, tell my
brother to divide the inheritance with me." Jesus replied,

> "Man, who made Me a judge or an arbitrator over you?"
> And He said to them, "Take heed and beware of cov-
> etousness, for one's life does not consist in the
> abundance of the things he possesses." (Luke 12:14–15)

• *Can you recall an experience in your life, or in the life of someone you know, in which hoarding led to loss rather than to increase or blessing? Can you recall an instance in which something that was hoarded was destroyed or lost before it could be of any use?*

_____

_____

What the Word Says

[Jesus taught,] "The ground of a certain rich man yielded plentifully. And he thought within himself, saying, 'What shall I do, since I have no room to store my crops?' So he said, 'I will do this: I will pull down my barns and build greater, and there I will store all my crops and my goods. And I will say to my soul, "Soul, you have many goods laid up for many years; take your ease; eat, drink, and be merry."' But God said to him, 'Fool! This night your soul will be required of you; then whose will those things be which you have provided?'"
So is he who lays up treasure for himself, and is not rich toward God." (Luke 12:16–21)

What the Word Says to Me

_____

_____

_____

_____

_____

_____

_____

_____

_____

_____

_____

_____

_____

_____

_____

_____

_____

_____

_____

3. Those Who Give Generously to the Lord Will Receive Generously from the Lord

Jesus said, "Give, and it will be given to you: good measure, pressed down, shaken together, and running over will be put into your bosom. For with the same measure that you use, it will be measured back to you" (Luke 6:38).

> • *What new insights do you have into Luke 6:38?*
>
> _____
>
> _____

Whatever we give—love, time, material substance, friendship, ideas, money, creativity, effort—the Lord returns to us *in the form of what we need.* The Lord not only gives us precisely what we need, but He gives it in overflowing supply. Furthermore, He very often gives to us through people other than those to whom we have given.

> • *Can you recall an experience in your life when God met your needs through someone other than a person to whom you had given generously?*
>
> _____
>
> _____

Are you looking today for God to pour out to you an *abundant, overflowing return* on your giving? Are you willing to give to God in a generous way and according to what is commanded in God's Word?

What the Word Says	What the Word Says to Me
[Jesus taught,] "With the same measure that you use, it will be measured back to you." (Luke 6:38)	
[The Lord said to His people through the prophet Malachi:] "Will a man rob God? Yet you have robbed Me! But you say,	

'In what way have we robbed You?'
In tithes and offerings.
You are cursed with a curse,
For you have robbed Me,
Even this whole nation.
Bring all the tithes into the
storehouse,
That there may be food
in My house,
And try Me now in this,"
Says the LORD of hosts,
"If I will not open for you the
windows of heaven
And pour out for you
such blessing
That there will not be room
enough to receive it.
And I will rebuke the devourer
for your sakes,
So that he will not destroy the
fruit of your ground,
Nor shall the vine fail to bear
fruit for you in the field,"
Says the LORD of hosts;
"And all nations will call you
blessed,
For you will be a delightful land,"
Says the LORD of hosts.
(Mal. 3:8–12)

• *In what ways are you feeling challenged in your spirit regarding your giving to God and receiving from God?*

4. We Are to Be Faithful Stewards of All That We Have Regardless of How Much We Have

Jesus said, "He who is faithful in what is least is faithful also in much; and he who is unjust in what is least is unjust also in much. Therefore if you have not been faithful in the unrighteous mammon, who will commit to your trust the true riches? And if you have not been faithful in what is another man's, who will give you what is your own?" (Luke 16:10–12).

•What new insights do you have into Luke 16:10–12?

_____

_____

When people hear a sermon about tithing or giving, too often they respond, "Well, I'll tithe when I make more money." The sad fact is that they won't. The person who is faithful in tithing on one dollar, two dollars, five dollars, and a hundred dollars will be the one faithful in tithing when he earns much more.

Material wealth is not limited to money, dollars, or stocks and bonds. Your house or apartment is a form of material wealth. The car you drive and the things you own are aspects of your material wealth. When we take good care of the things the Lord has already given to us, He can entrust us with His greater riches, which include inner riches such as spiritual leadership.

5. Our Stewardship Is Directly Related to What We Worship or What We Serve

Jesus said, "No servant can serve two masters; for either he will hate the one and love the other, or else he will be loyal to the one and despise the other. You cannot serve God and mammon" (Luke 16:13).

The thing that is at the center of your thinking or the center of your desire is the thing you worship—it is the thing you serve, the thing you admire and respect the most, the thing for which you long the most. Those who place financial gain as their top priority in life are people who have given money the place that belongs to God. They are guilty of idolatry.

The greedy person—the person who is never satisfied with the financial blessing he has been given—is a person who desires the "blessing" of money more than he desires the "Giver" of all blessings. He is a person who cannot be satisfied and who is never truly thankful for what the Lord has given.

> • *In your experience, can you recall a time or instance in which you found yourself serving something or someone other than God? What were the results? How did you feel?*

_____

_____

What the Word Says	What the Word Says to Me
For the love of money is a root of all kinds of evil, for which some have strayed from the faith in their greediness, and pierced themselves through with many sorrows. (1 Tim. 6:10)	----------------------------------- ----------------------------------- ----------------------------------- ----------------------------------- ----------------------------------- -----------------------------------
Those who desire to be rich fall into temptation and a snare, and into many foolish and harmful lusts which drown men in destruction and perdition. (1 Tim. 6:9)	----------------------------------- ----------------------------------- ----------------------------------- ----------------------------------- ----------------------------------- -----------------------------------

The more you earn and the more you acquire, the more you need to be in the Word of God, seeking direction and wisdom and guidance about how to *use* the money the Lord has given to you.

Through my years of ministry, I have seen a number of people prosper in their businesses and acquire small fortunes.

Unfortunately, some of these people didn't have any idea how to handle large sums of money, and they lost the fortunes they had acquired.

Others who became increasingly wealthy knew how to handle their money, but they lost sight of God's purposes in giving them money. Rather than use their money to support the work of the Lord and do good, they used their money for their own selfish pleasures. In the end, these people may not have lost their fortunes, but they lost sight of what truly mattered in life. They lost their peace of mind, their joy in the Lord, and their inner sense of fulfillment and satisfaction. They had money, but they were not genuinely successful.

Choose to be wise about money. It is a factor involved in success because it is a factor of our lives as a whole. But it is neither the definition of success nor should it ever be the foremost priority of our lives.

> • *What new insights do you have into the relationship between money and success?*
>
> _____
>
> _____
>
> • *In what ways are you feeling challenged in your spirit today?*
>
> _____
>
> _____

SEVEN

HURDLING THE ROADBLOCKS TO SUCCESS

Why do some people who set goals fail to reach them? Why does success seem to elude some people who truly *want* to be successful?

A wide variety of reasons have been suggested but I believe the true root reasons for a person to fail in fulfilling the God-given goals he has set for his life lie *inside* a person. They are not external, material, or circumstantial reasons.

Laying Aside Every Weight

Hebrews 12:1–2 gives us an important insight that can help us overcome the roadblocks that we encounter on our path toward success:

> Therefore we also, since we are surrounded by so great a cloud of witnesses, let us lay aside every weight, and the sin which so easily ensnares us, and let us run with endurance the race that is set before us, looking unto Jesus, the author and finisher of our faith, who for the joy that was set before Him endured the cross, despising the shame, and has sat down at the right hand of the throne of God.

The good news in this passage is that you are surrounded by a host of encouragers, both those who are living and those who have gone on to be with the Lord. There are countless saints of God who have lived successful lives in Christ Jesus—they can be, and should be, a great inspiration to us. Two of the greatest things you can do for yourself are (1) to read biographies of great Christian men and women, both those in history and those who are alive today, and (2) to associate with older and more mature Christians who are experiencing success God's way.

> • *In your life, who has been most encouraging to you that a Christian can live a successful life, God's way?*
>
> _____
>
> _____

The Lord Himself, of course, should always be our greatest encourager. He tells us in Hebrews 13:5, "I will never leave you nor forsake you." The Lord is present with us always to help us, teach us, guide us, comfort us, and empower us. He is the One who gives us the strength and ability to hurdle the roadblocks that lie in our path to success.

- *Weights.* Weights are those things that trouble us, weigh heavily on our minds, and cause us to be worried, frustrated, or discouraged.
- *Sins.* Sins are those things that entangle us and cause us to miss out on God's blessings and opportunities.

Both are things *we* must put down. Nobody else can strip these things from our lives. We must take charge and lay aside those things that hold us back from our pursuit of godly goals. We are the ones who must choose to run with endurance the race the Lord sets before us.

• *In your experience, have you found that certain things, habits, or associations became or are becoming "weights" to you? Are you being challenged in your spirit today to lay aside certain sins?*

_____

_____

• *What other insights do you have into Hebrews 12:1–2?*

_____

_____

Seven Roadblocks to Success

In this lesson we are going to focus on seven roadblocks that keep us back from godly success.

1. The Roadblock of Gripping Fear

A gripping fear is one that paralyzes us with feelings that we are threatened, unable, incapable, or inadequate. It is not a normal, natural fear, such as the fear of falling, or the fear that a child should have about walking out into busy traffic on a major highway. This is fear that keeps us bottled up and stagnant.

Gripping fears may cause us to become defensive and look for excuses about why we are not succeeding. These fears can cause us to want to flee from our goals or to dismiss our goals as being unimportant or invalid.

Faith is the opposite of fear. It is the solution for fear. In order to hurdle this roadblock, you are going to have to do things that build up your faith.

The first and best thing any of us can do to build up our faith is to get our eyes off our problem and off ourselves and, instead, onto Jesus. He is the One who is utterly reliable and who possesses all knowledge, authority, power, ability, wisdom, and strength. I encourage you to immerse yourself in reading and memorizing Scriptures that will build up your faith. Anytime a gripping fear takes hold of you, speak aloud faith-building verses. Ask the Lord to manifest the truth of these verses in your life.

What the Word Says	What the Word Says to Me
The LORD is my helper; I will not fear. What can man do to me? (Heb. 13:6)	
Fear not, for I am with you; Be not dismayed, for I am your God. I will strengthen you, Yes, I will help you, I will uphold you with My righteous right hand. Behold, all those who were incensed against you Shall be ashamed and disgraced; They shall be as nothing, And those who strive with you shall perish. You shall seek them and not find them— Those who contended with you. Those who war against you Shall be as nothing, As a nonexistent thing. For I, the LORD your God, will hold your right hand, Saying to you, "Fear not, I will help you." (Isa. 41:10–13)	

2. The Roadblock of Nagging Doubt

A success roadblock closely related to fear is doubt. Doubt is a lack of assurance. When we doubt, we become unsteady, tentative, and wavering in our pursuit of a goal. We may not become paralyzed or be put into "flight" mode as with fear, but we may become bogged down and fail to miss important opportunities for advancement.

Hebrews 11:6 tells us, "Without faith it is impossible to please Him, for he who comes to God must believe that He is, and that He is a rewarder of those who diligently seek Him."

How is it that we *please* God? By receiving His Son, Jesus Christ, as our Savior, and by obeying Him day by day. The exercise of our faith requires daily obedience to what God tells us to do, not only in His commandments, but in the pursuit of the goals He has designed for our lives.

One of the main reasons people doubt is because they lack understanding that God is with them always. Anytime you experience momentary doubt, I encourage you to get on your knees, open your Bible, and begin to read God's Word aloud back to God, saying, "Lord, this is what You have said in Your Word. I am trusting You to do this in my life."

> • *In your experience, have you had a struggle with nagging doubts? What has been most helpful to you in overcoming those doubts?*

_____

_____

What the Word Says	What the Word Says to Me
[Jesus taught,] "Have faith in God. For assuredly, I say to you, whoever says to this mountain, 'Be removed and be cast into the sea,' and does not doubt in his heart, but believes	_____ _____ _____ _____ _____ _____

that those things he says will
be done, he will have whatever
he says. Therefore I say to you,
whatever things you ask when
you pray, believe that you
receive them, and you will have
them." (Mark 11:22–24)

We walk by faith, not by sight.
(2 Cor. 5:7)

The life which I now live in the
flesh I live by faith in the Son
of God, who loved me and gave
Himself for me. (Gal. 2:20)

----

3. The Roadblock of Excuse-itis

Excuse-itis is an infection of self-justifications and excuses
that takes root and rots away at a person's *desire* to pursue godly
goals. It is the habit of offering an excuse at every turn for *not*
doing what a person knows to do. It is the cornerstone of the
"blame game"—blaming this person or that, this condition or
that situation, this lack or that inadequacy—in order to make
ourselves "feel better" about our failure to pursue godly goals.

Jesus told a parable about a rich man who went on a journey and entrusted his wealth to three servants. To one he gave
five talents, to another two talents, and to a third just one talent. When the master returned, he found that the first two
servants had doubled his money in his absence. The third servant, however, got into excuse-itis. He said, "Lord, I knew you
to be a hard man, reaping where you have not sown, and gath-
ering where you have not scattered seed. And I was afraid, and
went and hid your talent in the ground. Look, there you have
what is yours" (Matt. 25:24–25).

This servant attempted to blame his master for his failure to
do anything with the talent he had been given! The master

called this servant "wicked and lazy" and took the talent from him and gave it to the one who had produced ten talents.

Never try to blame another person for your failures. Redirect that energy into getting started on the pursuit of your God-given goals!

One of the best ways to overcome excuse-itis is to get involved in an accountability group or relationship. The support and prayers of others can be an encouragement to you, and also provide a "reality check" for you to keep you from playing the blame game.

What the Word Says	What the Word Says to Me
Pray for one another, that you may be healed. (James 5:16)	
For if anyone thinks himself to be something, when he is nothing, he deceives himself. But let each one examine his own work, and then he will have rejoicing in himself alone, and not in another. For each one shall bear his own load. (Gal. 6:3–5)	
[Note: This verse is also true for those who think they are nothing when they are something! They are also deceived. Part of examining our own work includes taking responsibility for our own work, so that whether it is good or bad, we are the foremost judges of what we do in the light of God's Word.]	

Comfort each other and edify
one another. (1 Thess. 5:11)

4. The Roadblock of Procrastination

Procrastination is putting off until tomorrow what you know you should do today. Two main types of people are prone to procrastination:

1. Perfectionists. The first type of person prone to procrastination is the perfectionist. The perfectionist is not simply a person who does the best he can at the things he undertakes—the perfectionist feels *driven* to do everything *perfectly*. The perfectionist, therefore, often procrastinates from undertaking projects because he anticipates the possibility of failure or the inevitability of falling short of perfection.

2. Discomfort-dodgers. The second type of person prone to procrastination is the "discomfort-dodger." This person knows that accomplishing goals takes effort, energy, saying "no" to frivolous pleasures and fleshly lusts—all of which can lead to discomfort from a life of ease.

If you are a perfectionist or a discomfort-dodger, ask the Lord to help you overcome these detrimental traits. The fact is, nobody is perfect except God. God knows all about your imperfections and still chooses to reside in you by the power of the Holy Spirit to help you overcome your imperfections. The perfecting work is *His*, not yours. The fact is also that God will *help* you overcome emotional laziness, but you must do the work of setting rewards for yourself, motivating yourself, and choosing to expend energy and effort. God will do for you what you *cannot* do, but not what you *choose not* to do.

One of the best ways to overcome procrastination is to set a limited number of very specific, doable daily goals. Write them down, and every morning ask the Lord to help you accomplish the things you have identified on your list.

• In your experience, have you encountered the roadblock of procrastination? What did you do to hurdle this roadblock?

_____

_____

What the Word Says	What the Word Says to Me
Take heed to the ministry which you have received in the Lord, that you may fulfill it. (Col. 4:17)	---------------------------------- ---------------------------------- ---------------------------------- ----------------------------------
See then that you walk circumspectly, not as fools but as wise, redeeming the time. (Eph. 5:15)	---------------------------------- ---------------------------------- ---------------------------------- ----------------------------------

5. The Roadblock of Insatiable Greed

Greed is an insatiable hunger or craving for acquiring more than a person needs. Greed has no bottom to it. It can never be satisfied. Nothing is ever "enough."

How does greed become a stumbling block? Greed functions in the natural world. It causes a person to want more and more of what is material and financial. The greedy person pursues just one more dollar, one more acquisition, one more dress or suit, one more fix or pill, one more piece of property. The more the person pursues that "one more thing," the less the person has eyes for true spiritual concerns and riches.

The pursuit of the natural world eventually supersedes all desire to pursue the things of God. When that happens, a person's life falls out of balance, and genuine, God-given goals take a backseat. No person who is bound by the natural world can be truly successful in God's eyes. The Lord's desire is always that we hunger and thirst for those things that *He* establishes as good and desirable for us and for others around us.

Furthermore, there is no way that a greedy person can practice greed without stepping on somebody's toes or alienating other people. The greedy person tends to wall off other people whom he perceives as being in competition for what he desires. The greedy person also tends to misuse, abuse, and take advantage of other people in his unending quest to put more and more worldly goods under his control.

One of the best remedies for greed is to begin to give sacrificially—to give away a possession you value highly or to give to the degree that you eliminate a luxury you have come to think of as a necessity.

What the Word Says

Beware, and be on your guard against every form of greed; for not even when one has an abundance does his life consist of his possessions.
(Luke 12:15 NASB)

Do not let immorality or any impurity or greed even be named among you, as is proper among saints. (Eph. 5:3 NASB)

[Jesus taught,] "Blessed are those who hunger and thirst for righteousness,
For they shall be filled."
(Matt. 5:6)

Command those who are rich in this present age not to be haughty, nor to trust in uncertain riches but in the living God, who gives us richly all things to enjoy. Let them do

What the Word Says to Me

----

good, that they be rich in good	....
works, ready to give, willing to	....
share, storing up for them-	....
selves a good foundation for	....
the time to come, that they	....
may lay hold on eternal life.	....
(1 Tim. 6:17–19)	....

6. The Roadblock of Sin

Another way of stating this roadblock is "the violation of our conscience." Your conscience acts as an internal alarm system in your spirit and soul that you either have entered into or are about to enter into a "sin zone." Your conscience warns you against dangers that can lead to moral and spiritual destruction.

The more a person violates his conscience, the less regard he has for the warning signals of his conscience. His understanding of what is right and wrong becomes cloudy and uncertain. His ability to discern evil becomes inoperative. Such a person is more prone to embark on detours that can lead him away from genuine success.

- *In your life, have you every had an experience in which you knowingly violated the warning signals from your own conscience? What were the results? How did you feel?*

_____

_____

What the Word Says	**What the Word Says to Me**
Some will depart from the faith . . . speaking lies in hypocrisy, having their own conscience seared with a hot iron. (1 Tim. 4:1–2)	....
Examine yourselves as to whether you are in the faith.	....

Test yourselves. Do you not
know yourselves, that Jesus
Christ is in you? (2 Cor.
13:5)

Do not let sin reign in your
mortal body, that you should
obey it in its lusts. And do not
present your members as
instruments of unrighteousness
to sin, but present yourselves
to God as being alive from the
dead, and your members as
instruments of righteousness
to God. (Rom. 6:12–13)

For the wages of sin is death,
but the gift of God is eternal
life in Christ Jesus our Lord.
(Rom. 6:23)

7. The Roadblock of Slothfulness

Slothfulness is a big term for "lazy." In the Bible, being slothful is contrasted to being industrious or working diligently. The
slothful person is a person who does as little as possible, and who
seeks to get by in life with minimal effort, minimal expenditure
of creativity and energy, and minimal involvement with others.
None of these behaviors are associated with godly success!

The pursuit of godly goals takes energy. The building of godly
relationships takes diligence and effort. The pursuit of godly
success takes an expenditure of time and creativity.

If you struggle with slothfulness, I encourage you to reeval-
uate your goals. Perhaps you haven't identified goals that have
a sense of God-given urgency about them. Perhaps you haven't
identified goals toward which you feel a strong compulsion to
act. Set goals that motivate you. And then insist within yourself

that you will get up each morning and pursue them to the best of your ability!

• *In your life, have you ever struggled with slothfulness? What motivated you to act?*

_____

_____

What the Word Says

He who is slothful in his work
Is a brother to him who is a
great destroyer. (Prov. 18:9)

Because of laziness the building decays,
And through idleness of hands
the house leaks. (Eccl. 10:18)

I went by the field of the lazy
man,
And by the vineyard of the
man devoid of understanding;
And there it was, all overgrown
with thorns;
Its surface was covered with
nettles;
Its stone wall was broken down.
When I saw it, I considered it
well;
I looked on it and received
instruction:
A little sleep, a little slumber,
A little folding of the hands
to rest;
So shall your poverty come like

What the Word Says to Me

----

a prowler,
And your need like an armed
man. (Prov. 24:30–34)

Keeping Your Sights on the Future Ahead

Never let a roadblock cloud your ultimate desire or vision of godly success. Don't allow yourself to become so immersed in solving an immediate problem or overcoming an immediate obstacle that you lose sight of the big picture of your most important goals. Ask the Lord to help you keep your focus on Him and on what He desires for you to be and do in your life.

Ask the Holy Spirit to *help* you as you take action to remove or to hurdle these roadblocks to your success. The Holy Spirit will not override your personal will or sovereignly remove these "weights and sins" from your path, but when you invite Him to help you, He will do so!

• *What new insights do you have into the reasons you may not have been as successful as you desired? What new insights do you have into the inner roadblocks that you need to remove from your path toward godly success?*

_____

_____

• *How do you feel about the "work" that lies ahead for you to do in pursuing success?*

_____

_____

• *In what ways are you feeling challenged in your spirit to take immediate action steps?*

_____

_____

EIGHT

SUCCESSFUL ATTITUDES AND IDEAS

Have you ever stopped to think that everything around you first began with a *thought*? It either began as a thought in the mind of God or as a thought in the mind of a man or woman. What an awesome, creative power lies in our *minds*, the organ of thinking and the seat of opinions and attitudes.

Few of us ever stop to consider fully the power of our own thoughts and attitudes, but the Bible proclaims about a man, "As he thinks in his heart, so is he" (Prov. 23:7).

How is it that we are to think in order to become the person God desires for us to be? We are to think as Jesus thinks. The apostle Paul wrote, "Let this mind be in you which was also in Christ Jesus" (Phil. 2:5).

The Bible is very specific about the "thought life" we are to have as believers—the thought life that leads to our *being* who the Lord created us to be, and which leads to our *doing* what He created us to do.

What the Word Says	What the Word Says to Me
Therefore put to death your members which are on the earth: fornication, uncleanness, passion, evil desire, and covetousness, which is idolatry. Because of these things the wrath of God is coming upon the sons of disobedience, in which you yourselves once walked when you lived in them. But now you yourselves are to put off all these: anger, wrath, malice, blasphemy, filthy language out of your mouth. Do not lie to one another, since you have put off the old man with his deeds, and have put on the new man who is renewed in knowledge according to the image of Him who created him. (Col. 3:5–10)	---
Brethren, whatever things are true . . . noble . . . just . . . pure . . . lovely . . . of good report, if there is any virtue and if there is anything praise-worthy—meditate on these things. (Phil. 4:8)	---

Monitoring Your Own Thought Life

There are four main areas of your thought life that are important for you to monitor diligently.

1. What Are You Thinking About *Yourself?* How Do You Feel About *Yourself?*

How you think or feel about yourself is going to be projected into the way you behave, including the choices you make and the way you approach problems. A negative perception will manifest itself in your speech, usually in the form of criticism and negative comments. It will manifest itself in your body language, perhaps in the form of a limp handshake, a slouchy walk, a drooped head, downcast eyes, or a sad expression. It will manifest itself in the way you work—if you don't value yourself, you are more likely to produce less work or lower quality.

When you change the way you think about yourself, very often you change the way others think about you, and that, in turn, often changes the circumstances and situations in which you find yourself.

• *How do you feel about yourself? What do you think of yourself?*

_____

_____

What the Word Says	What the Word Says to Me
I will praise You, for I am fear-fully and wonderfully made; Marvelous are Your works, And that my soul knows very well. My frame was not hidden from You, When I was made in secret, And skillfully wrought in the lowest parts of the earth. Your eyes saw my substance, being yet unformed. And in Your book they all were written,	_____ _____ _____ _____ _____ _____ _____ _____ _____ _____ _____ _____ _____

The days fashioned for me,
When as yet there were none
of them.
How precious also are Your
thoughts to me, O God!
How great is the sum of them!
(Ps. 139:14–17)

2. What Are You Thinking and Feeling About Your *Circumstances*?

How do you feel about your home . . . your place of employment . . . your neighborhood? The way you think and feel about your environment is going to affect how you behave, treat your possessions, schedule your time, manage your money, and communicate with others who share your home, workplace, or community. Your perceptions about your environment will alter your perceptions about your own potential for success.

• *How do you feel—what do you think—about your home, workplace, and neighborhood?*

What the Word Says

[The men Moses sent to spy out the land of Canaan returned and said to Moses,] "We went to the land where you sent us. It truly flows with milk and honey, and this is its fruit. Nevertheless the people who dwell in the land are strong; the cities are fortified and very large; moreover we

What the Word Says to Me

saw the descendants of Anak there. The Amalekites dwell in the land of the South; the Hittites, the Jebusites, and the Amorites dwell in the mountains; and the Canaanites dwell by the sea and along the banks of the Jordan" . . . "The land through which we have gone as spies is a land that devours its inhabitants, and all the people whom we saw in it are men of great stature . . . we were like grasshoppers in our own sight, and so we were in their sight." So all the congregation lifted up their voices and cried, and the people wept that night. (Num. 13:27–29, 32–33, 14:1)

[Note: Read Numbers 14 to see what happened as a result of what the people THOUGHT about the Promised Land.]

3. What Are You Thinking About *Other People*?

Are there certain classes or groups of people that you don't like "in general"? Your thoughts and feelings about other people determine your relationships. People tend to cluster around commonly held beliefs or a mutually held perspective on life. To a great extent, what you think influences your choice of friends, spouse, business associates, and mentors. All of these key relationships, in turn, impact your progress toward becoming and doing what God desires for you to be and do.

Especially consider the thoughts and feelings you have toward your family and children. Do you see them as a gift of God to your life?

- *How do you feel about other people? What prejudices are you willing to admit? What is the attitude that you believe others perceive in you?*

_____

_____

- *What specific thoughts and feelings do you have about your spouse and children?*

_____

_____

What the Word Says

Therefore if there is any consolation in Christ, if any comfort of love, if any fellowship of the Spirit, if any affection and mercy, fulfill my joy by being like-minded, having the same love, being of one accord, of one mind. Let nothing be done through selfish ambition or conceit, but in lowliness of mind let each esteem others better than himself. Let each of you look out not only for his own interests, but also for the interests of others. (Phil. 2:1–4)

Be kind to one another, tenderhearted, forgiving one another, even as God in Christ forgave you. (Eph. 4:32)

What the Word Says to Me

_____

_____

_____

_____

_____

_____

_____

_____

_____

_____

_____

_____

_____

_____

_____

_____

_____

_____

_____

There is neither Jew nor Greek, there is neither slave nor free, there is neither male nor female; for you are all one in Christ Jesus. (Gal. 3:28)	--
	--
	--
	--
	--

4. What Do You Think About *God*? How Do You Feel Toward *God*?

Your thoughts and feelings determine your relationship with God. If you think of God as a judge who is keeping score continually about your behavior and judging you guilty and unworthy at every turn, you are far less likely to want to spend time with God in prayer or to meditate on His Word. On the other hand, if you think of God as a loving Father, you are much more likely to desire to spend time reading His Word and communicating with Him.

Your thoughts are directly related to your faith.

> • *How do you feel about God today—honestly? What ten words would you use to describe God? Your choice of words reflects your feelings and thoughts about God.*

What the Word Says	**What the Word Says to Me**
Hear, O Israel: The LORD our God, the LORD is one! You shall love the LORD your God with all your heart, with all your soul, and with all your strength. (Deut. 6:4–5)	--
	--
	--
	--
	--
God spoke all these words, saying: "I am the LORD your God, who brought you out of	--
	--
	--

the land of Egypt, out of the
house of bondage. You shall
have no other gods before
Me . . . For I, the LORD your
God, am a jealous God,
visiting the iniquity of the
fathers upon the children to
the third and fourth genera-
tions of those who hate Me,
but showing mercy to thou-
sands, to those who love Me
and keep My commandments.
(Ex. 20:1–6)

God's Challenge to Think Positively

Is a negative response to the life God sets before us ever war-
ranted? No. Of all the people we encounter in the New
Testament, the apostle Paul probably had the greatest reason to
develop negative thinking. He encountered a host of negative
situations and responses to his preaching of the gospel. The last
years of his life were spent in confinement. Even so, read what
Paul wrote to the Philippians from his prison chamber in Rome:

> But I rejoiced in the Lord greatly that now at last your
> care for me has flourished again; though you surely did
> care, but you lacked opportunity. Not that I speak in
> regard to need, for I have learned in whatever state I am,
> to be content: I know how to be abased, and I know
> how to abound. Everywhere and in all things I have
> learned both to be full and to be hungry, both to
> abound and to suffer need. I can do all things through
> Christ who strengthens me . . .
> I am full, having received from Epaphroditus the things
> sent from you, a sweet-smelling aroma, an acceptable sac-
> rifice, well pleasing to God. And my God shall supply

all your need according to His riches in glory by Christ Jesus. (Phil. 4:10–13, 18–19)

Even though he was in prison, Paul wrote with an attitude of thanksgiving, encouragement, contentment, and faith in the Lord to supply not only his needs, but the needs of the Philippians. Paul was a man who chose to think *God's* way—that adversity does not mean defeat—and to believe for God's highest and best at all times. He was a man who chose to remain positive and hopeful about his future and the future of others.

Was Paul an idealist or a fantasizer? No. He was a realist. He didn't *deny* that he faced problems or that he was in prison. Paul recognized, however, as we must, that life is never totally negative or totally positive. We can choose which side of life to think about, to believe for, and to aim at.

• *What additional insights do you have into the verses above from Philippians 4?*

———————————————————————————

———————————————————————————

Lining Up Our Thinking and Feeling with God's Word

We each are challenged to line up our thinking and our attitudes with God's Word. Many of us have been "programmed" to think and to respond to life in ways that are contrary to God's best. Paul wrote to the Romans:

I beseech you therefore, brethren, by the mercies of God, that you present your bodies a living sacrifice, holy, acceptable to God, which is your reasonable service. And do not be conformed to this world, but be transformed by the renewing of your mind, that you may prove what is that good and acceptable and perfect will of God. (Rom. 12:1–2)

The transformation of our minds to be conformed to the things of God is our responsibility, nobody else's. The word for "renewing" the mind is a word that means "to make a change." We each must choose to change the way we think so that our thoughts and feelings are in line with God's truth.

•*What insights do you have into this passage?*

—————————————————————————

—————————————————————————

• *Reflecting back over your life since you accepted Jesus Christ as your Savior, identify several specific ways in which you have been "transformed by the renewing of your mind" so that you have a better understanding of what is pleasing to God.*

—————————————————————————

—————————————————————————

What the Word Says	**What the Word Says to Me**
Your word I have hidden in my heart, That I might not sin against You. (Ps. 119:11)	....
Set your mind on things above, not on things on the earth. (Col. 3:2)	....

•*What new insights do you have into the impact that your thoughts and emotions have on your pursuit of success?*

—————————————————————————

—————————————————————————

• *In what ways are you feeling challenged in your spirit to change your attitudes or thoughts?*

—————————————————————————

—————————————————————————

NINE

A SUCCESSFUL USE OF TIME

S uccess can not be separated from a wise use of time. Many people attempt to be successful without any thought to time, but those who truly attain success are those who have learned to respect and honor time in their lives. The apostle Paul had this to say about time management:

> See then that you walk circumspectly, not as fools but as wise, redeeming the time, because the days are evil. (Eph. 5:15–16)

To "walk circumspectly" is to be careful in the way one lives. It is to live an *intentional* life—not a life of following every whim, but to pursue a course in life that is purposeful. It is to recognize that *moments are important.*

To the Galatians, Paul wrote, "Let us not grow weary while doing good . . . as we have opportunity, let us do good to all" (Gal. 6:9–10). The word for "opportunity" means "making the most of your time." Time and opportunity are vitally linked to success.

> • *Reflect back over your life. Cite instances when you have been keenly aware of making the most of a particular time. Can*

you cite experiences in which you did not give due regard to time? What were the results?

_____

_____

Time Is a Gift from God

God has given to each of us a length of time on this earth in which to fulfill His plan and purpose for us. Time is a *gift* to us.

Our time on this earth is an unknown quantity. We cannot regain lost moments or relive hours. It is up to each of us to ask the Lord, "How can I use my talents and gifts from You in the time you are giving to me in order to best fulfill Your purpose?"

An Urgency About Time

Throughout the Bible we find references to the brevity of life and the swift movement of our lives through time. Rather than be discouraged about the brevity of the time we have on this earth, we should be all the more eager to make the most of every moment.

What the Word Says	What the Word Says to Me
What is your life? It is even a vapor that appears for a little time and then vanishes away. (James 4:14)	-- -- -- --
[Job said,] "My days are swifter than a weaver's shuttle." (Job 7:6)	-- -- --

A Call to Manage Time Wisely

The Lord expects us to manage our time wisely: creating a balance between work and rest . . . setting aside times for family and for being with Him, and making prayer and Bible reading a priority in our daily schedules. No person is asked to be a workaholic. To lead a nonstop work life is to live in disobedience to God's commandment: "Six days you shall labor and do all your work, but the seventh day is the Sabbath of the LORD your God" (Ex. 20:9–10).

Nothing is a waste of time if it is part of a balanced *plan* for time—a plan that is developed for the fulfillment of God's purposes and for maximum usefulness, productivity, and efficiency in the use of a person's talents and gifts.

Five Keys to Good Time Management

The Bible gives us five important and practical principles for good time management:

1. Seek God's Guidance

God has ordained for you a series of good works to accomplish. Ask the Lord each morning to help you identify the good works that He has planned for you on that particular day. Ask the Lord to show you *how* and *when* and *to whom* you might minister by using the good gifts and talents He has given you.

What the Word Says	What the Word Says to Me
We are His workmanship, created in Christ Jesus for good works, which God prepared beforehand that we should walk in them. (Eph. 2:10)	----------------------------------- ----------------------------------- ----------------------------------- ----------------------------------- -----------------------------------
He no longer should live the rest of his time in the flesh for the lusts of men, but for the will of God. For we have spent enough of our past lifetime in doing the will of the Gentiles . . . As each one has received a	----------------------------------- ----------------------------------- ----------------------------------- ----------------------------------- ----------------------------------- ----------------------------------- -----------------------------------

gift, minister it to one another, as good stewards of the mani-fold grace of God. (1 Peter 4:2–3, 10)

----

2. Plan Your Schedule

Months can go by without your making any progress toward the fulfillment of your God-given goals *if you don't plan your schedule* and set your God-given goals and dreams into the context of deadlines.

Ask the Lord to show you *how* to set your schedule for any given day, week, or year to allow for a good balance of work and rest, alone time and family time, input and output.

As we make plans, we must always remain flexible to specific ways in which the Lord may redirect our paths. James said,

> Come now, you who say, "Today or tomorrow we will go to such and such a city, spend a year there, buy and sell, and make a profit"; whereas you do not know what will happen tomorrow . . . Instead you ought to say, "If the Lord wills, we shall live and do this or that." (James 4:13–15)

• *What new insights do you have into this passage from James?*

_____

_____

3. Stay Organized

Continually searching for missing documents or items is a waste of time. Stay organized as you work. Throughout the Bible, we find numerous references about doing things and maintaining things in an orderly fashion. (See Exodus 40:1–16 as an example.) Organization is a key to efficiency. And efficiency is an important ingredient related to the *rate of progress* you can make toward achieving your God-given goals.

Consider what happens to a flock of sheep when no shepherd is present to "organize" them and keep them together in an orderly fashion:

> They were scattered because there was no shepherd; and they became food for all the beasts of the field when they were scattered. (Ezek. 34:5)

A similar thing happens to us when we fail to organize the tasks, events, and projects that are put into our care. A lack of organization can lead to loss, struggle, and emotional turmoil.

What the Word Says	What the Word Says to Me
For God is not the author of confusion but of peace . . . Let all things be done decently and in order. (1 Cor. 14:33, 40)	----------------------------------
Direct my steps by Your word, And let no iniquity have dominion over me. (Ps. 119:133)	----------------------------------
[*See Luke 9:10–17. Note in particular verse 14 and the "order" that Jesus established for this group.*]	----------------------------------

4. Eliminate the Unimportant

Many things are not *worthy* of your time. Let them go! Other things are vitally important to your purpose on the earth. Emphasize them!

I am absolutely convinced that if a person will choose to lay aside all those things that result in a derailment or a detour from the main purpose God has for a person's life, that person will be highly productive, and in turn, more efficient, and in the end, very successful. The Lord said to Joshua about His plan for Joshua's life, "Do not turn from it to the right hand or to the left, that you may prosper wherever you go" (Josh. 1:7).

Stay focused in your use of time and your pursuit of your goals!

What the Word Says	What the Word Says to Me
[Jesus taught this about a life that is "focused" on what is truly important,] "Narrow is the gate and difficult is the way which leads to life, and there are few who find it." (Matt. 7:14)	....
I have this against you, that you have left your first love. Remember therefore from where you have fallen; repent and do the first works. (Rev. 2:4–5)	....

5. Review Each Day

At the close of a day, review the way in which you have spent your time. Evaluate your schedule. Compare what you did with what you intended to do. Ask yourself:

- Did I make good use of my time?
- Did I procrastinate?
- Was I able to maintain concentration?
- Did I engage in activities that truly were priorities?
- Did I make progress (even a little) toward the accomplishment of my God-given goals?

What the Word Says	What the Word Says to Me
May the Lord give you understanding in all things. (2 Tim. 2:7)	....

Therefore know this day, and
consider it in your heart.
(Deut. 4:39)

Thus says the LORD of hosts,
"Consider your ways!"
(Hag. 1:5)

A Disciplined, Diligent Life Leads to Success

Ultimately, the wise use of time is a mark of a disciplined life. And a disciplined life is a life that, when focused on godly goals, results in success. In the Bible, a disciplined life is often called a "diligent life." As you read through the verses below, ask the Lord to reveal to you ways in which you need to be more diligent in your use of time.

What the Word Says	What the Word Says to Me
The hand of the diligent makes rich. (Prov. 10:4)	
The hand of the diligent will rule. (Prov. 12:24)	
The soul of the diligent shall be made rich. (Prov. 13:4)	
The plans of the diligent lead surely to plenty. (Prov. 21:5)	

As you put the five principles of good time management covered in this study into action on a daily, consistent basis, you are going to discover that you are not only growing in self-esteem, but that you are moving closer and closer to the fulfillment of God's purpose for your life. You will not only be *doing* what the Lord has set before you to do, but you will be in the process of *becoming* the disciplined person that the Lord desires for you to be.

• *What new insights do you have into the relationship between success and the wise use of time?*

_____

_____

• *In what ways are you feeling challenged in your spirit?*

_____

_____

TEN

PERSISTING UNTIL YOU SUCCEED

I have never met a person who didn't want to succeed at *something*. At the same time, I have met very few people who are succeeding at *everything*—or even most things—they believe to be God-given goals for their life. Most people seem to allow something, or someone, to deter them, disappoint them, dissuade them, or discourage them from *persisting* in the pursuit of their goals.

God's plan and purpose for you is an *ever-growing plan and purpose*. You will never fully arrive at all you can be; you will never do all that you are capable of doing. But each day we are called to *continue to press* toward becoming what God sets out as the character pattern for our lives: the fullness of the maturity of Christ Jesus. We are to *continue to endure* in our faith journey toward the goals God has put before us. There is no justification in God's Word for giving up.

Persistence is the one trait you are going to find in the life of every person who has achieved something worthwhile in life. It is a combination of strong desire and willpower. It is the capacity to continue on course in the face of all types of difficulties, obstacles, and problems . . . and not quit. Persistence is raw determination to move forward rather than to stop or slide backward.

• *In your life or in the life of someone you know, can you cite an experience in which sheer persistence made the difference between success or failure?*

Is Quitting Ever Justified?

Is there ever a good enough reason to quit persisting in the pursuit of your goals? No.

The apostle Paul wrote this to the Corinthians:

> Are they ministers of Christ? . . . I am more: in labors more abundant, in stripes above measure, in prisons more frequently, in deaths often. From the Jews five times I received forty stripes minus one. Three times I was beaten with rods; once I was stoned; three times I was shipwrecked; a night and a day I have been in the deep; in journeys often, in perils of waters, in perils of robbers, in perils of my own countrymen, in perils of the Gentiles, in perils in the city, in perils in the wilderness, in perils in the sea, in perils among false brethren; in weariness and toil, in sleeplessness often, in hunger and thirst, in fastings often, in cold and nakedness—besides the other things, what comes upon me daily: my deep concern for all the churches. (2 Cor. 11:23–28)

Is there any person alive today who has gone through so much hardship, pain, and difficulty in the pursuit of his goal? If anybody had a justifiable reason to give up, Paul did. Yet, there's no indication in any of his letters that Paul ever quit pressing toward his goals. God calls us to pursue our goals *regardless* of outer circumstances.

• *What insights do you have into 2 Corinthians 11:23–28? How did you feel as you read this passage?*

Factors That Impact Persistence

Several factors impact how persistent we will be in pursuing godly success:

- Focus—Our goals must be well-defined.
- God-given—We must have certainty that God has helped us set our goals.
- High value—We must see great value in accomplishing our goals, either for our own selves or for the benefit of others.
- Love factor—When our goals are directly related to someone we love and want to help, we are much more likely to persist in pursuing them.

Focused goals that have a clearly defined, eternal benefit to someone we love are very motivating!

Jesus gave several parables in which persistence was a key factor. In Luke 15 we read these words of Jesus:

> What man of you, having a hundred sheep, if he loses one of them, does not leave the ninety-nine in the wilderness, and go after the one which is lost until he finds it? And when he has found it, he lays it on his shoulders, rejoicing . . . Or what woman, having ten silver coins, if she loses one coin, does not light a lamp, sweep the house, and search carefully until she finds it? . . . Likewise, I say to you, there is joy in the presence of the angels of God over one sinner who repents. (4–5, 8, 10)

- *What new insights regarding persistence do you have after reading these two parables?*

———————————————————————

———————————————————————

No allowances are made in the Scriptures for "circumstances," "situations," or "retirement." We are to continue to pursue

God's goals for our lives every day of our lives, regardless of external factors.

What the Word Says	**What the Word Says to Me**
The love of Christ compels us. (2 Cor. 5:14)	....
Now it came to pass, when the time had come for Him to be received up, that He steadfastly set His face to go to Jerusalem. (Luke 9:51)	....
[Jesus said,] "No one, having put his hand to the plow, and looking back, is fit for the kingdom of God." (Luke 9:62)	....
[Note: Read this entire parable for a greater understanding of the context for this statement by Jesus.]	....

• *What is it today that is compelling you to persist in pursuing your goals?*

What about Striving?

There are those who claim that we are to cease all striving and to "rest" in the Lord (see Ps. 46:10; 37:7). Do these admonitions mean we are not to persist or to press on with diligence and steadfastness? No. These verses about resting in the Lord are related to putting our trust in the Lord. We are to rest in Him completely, trusting Him with our whole heart.

Did Jesus struggle and strive to make things happen? No. He trusted the Father. But did Jesus continue to pursue the

Father's goals for His life? Absolutely yes—all the way to the cross.

What the Word Says	**What the Word Says to Me**
Ruth said:	
"Entreat me not to leave you,	
Or to turn back from following	
after you;	
For wherever you go, I will go;	
And wherever you lodge,	
I will lodge;	
Your people shall be my people,	
And your God, my God.	
Where you die, I will die.	
And there will I be buried.	
The LORD do so to me, and	
more also,	
If anything but death parts you	
and me."	
When she [Naomi] saw that	
she was determined to go with	
her, she stopped speaking to	
her [to try to convince her to	
stay behind]. (Ruth 1:16–18)	
I am with you in spirit, rejoicing	
to see your good order and the	
steadfastness of your faith in	
Christ. As you therefore have	
received Christ Jesus the Lord,	
so walk in Him, rooted and built	
up in Him and established in the	
faith . . . abounding in it with	
thanksgiving. (Col. 2:5–7)	

Beware lest you also fall from
your own steadfastness, being
led away with the error of the
wicked. (2 Peter 3:17)

Why Persistence Is Required

Persistence is required if we are going to overcome certain
things that come into the life of every person from time to
time:

- *Discouragement.* We must persist in pursuing God's
  success for us even when we don't see much being
  accomplished or our efforts seem futile.
- *Failures and Mistakes.* All of us fail and make mistakes from time to time. We live in a fallen world,
  and there's no getting away from the inevitability
  of error. We must learn from our failures and move
  on, determined to act more wisely in the future.
- *Weariness.* We must persist even when we become
  physically and emotionally tired. Take a rest, but
  don't quit!

- *Recall experiences in which you felt discouraged, failed, or felt
  weary. What did you do to renew your motivation to pursue
  your goals in life?*

Five Principles Related to Persistence

We must always keep in mind several principles that pertain
to persistence:

1. *A person is not a failure just because he fails.* The difference
between an unsuccessful and a successful person is this: The
successful person keeps getting up each time he is knocked

down. You aren't a failure until you give up.

> • *Recall in your own life an experience in which you initially failed, but were later successful.*

_____

_____

2. A "test" does not mean that we are to stop pursuing a goal. A **test is** an opportunity to learn a valuable lesson on your way **to reaching** your goals. It is not a "stop" sign, but very often a **"yield more** to the Lord" sign, a "caution" sign, or a "return **to the** main road" sign!

3. In every failure, you'll find a seed of equivalent success. Choose to learn something from every mistake you make. Some of the most valuable lessons you will learn in life relate to "what doesn't work" or "what not to do."

What the Word Says	**What the Word Says to Me**
Blessed is the man who endures temptation; for when he has been approved, he will receive the crown of life which the Lord has promised to those who love Him. (James 1:12)	----------------------------------- ----------------------------------- ----------------------------------- ----------------------------------- ----------------------------------- -----------------------------------
My brethren, count it all joy when you fall into various trials, knowing that the testing of your faith produces patience. But let patience have its perfect work, that you may be perfect and complete, lacking nothing. (James 1:2–4)	----------------------------------- ----------------------------------- ----------------------------------- ----------------------------------- ----------------------------------- ----------------------------------- -----------------------------------
Take the helmet of salvation, and the sword of the Spirit,	----------------------------------- -----------------------------------

which is the word of God;

praying always with all prayer

and supplication in the Spirit,

being watchful to this end with

all perseverance. (Eph. 6:17–18)

4. *Bury your failures.* Don't frame your failures or keep revisiting them with remorse. Bury them and move on. If forgiveness is required, ask God to forgive you and ask others to forgive you. But then forgive yourself and get busy again in the pursuit of your God-given goals.

5. *Be quick to forgive others.* A person can get so caught up in the "blame game" or in scheming revenge that he loses all momentum in the pursuit of his goals. We each are responsible for our own actions, responses, and feelings. And there is never any justification in God's Word for hurting someone else, harboring unforgiveness, or taking vengeance in our own hands. Ultimately, the "blame game" hurts us more than it hurts others.

What the Word Says

What the Word Says to Me

[Jesus said,] "Forgive, and you will be forgiven." (Luke 6:37)

[Jesus said,] "If you forgive men their trespasses, your heavenly Father will also forgive you. But if you do not forgive men their trespasses, neither will your Father forgive your trespasses." (Matt. 6:14–15)

[Jesus said,] "Judge not, that you be not judged. For with what judgment you judge, you will be judged; and with the

measure you use, it will be
measured back to you."
(Matthew 7:1–2)

Keep Your Eyes on the Goal!

Periodically revisit your goals. Recall to your own mind the reasons your goals were important to you and to God. Rekindle your passion for reaching your God-given goals.

Refuse to listen to negative criticism. Good advice, rooted in a desire to see you succeed, and to do so with as few errors as possible, is highly valuable. But criticism—a tearing down of your idea, an effort to diminish the value of your goal, or an effort to thwart a good cause, service, or production of a good product—should never be heeded. Listen to what *God* says about you.

Surround yourself with people who will encourage you. You'll find it much easier to persist in the pursuit of your goals if you are surrounded by people who are encouraging you onward and who believe, as you do, that God is with you and God will help you.

Remember always that God never gives up on you. He does not waver from His purposes and plans. Paul wrote to the Philippians, "He who has begun a good work in you will complete it until the day of Jesus Christ" (Phil. 1:6). God is never going to give up on the perfecting work He has started in you.

Did God give up on you when you were a sinner? No.

Did God give up on you when you blew it and failed in your witness? No.

Did God give up on you when you strayed from Him and began to pursue your own desires and lusts? No.

Did God give up on you when you gave up in discouragement on the goals He gave you? No.

Will God ever give up on you? No!

God is always ready and eager to help you begin again, to

start over, and to make another attempt. Turn to Him and receive the help He so generously offers.

•*What new insights do you have into the need for persistence if you are to reach your God-given goals?*

_____

_____

• *In what ways are you feeling challenged in your spirit?*

_____

_____

CONCLUSION

WELL-ORDERED STEPS

One of the most important marks of Christian maturity is an ongoing and continual recognition that the Lord is the One who makes possible all good things in our lives. It is the mature believer who proclaims in all circumstances, "Every good and perfect gift comes from the Father" (see James 1:17).

Even when things seem dark, times are tough, or life seems unsettled, we can know with assurance that God is in charge of our lives and He *is* working all things together for our good. The Bible tells us,

> The steps of a good man are ordered by the LORD,
> And He delights in his way. (Ps. 37:23)

In good times and bad, on mediocre days and exhilarating days, in periods of joy and periods of heavy toil, our stance before the Lord must be, "God, You're in charge. God, I have no success other than what You help me achieve."

Trust God today to order each step you take toward the success He desires for you. Trust Him to order your steps and arrange all the details of your journey as you walk in faith. If you are walking along God's chosen path for you, and you are trusting Him to order each step, you *will* experience success—God's way!